THE MANY GODS ANTHOLOGIES
VOLUME 1: **HEKATE**

THE MANY GODS ANTHOLOGIES
Volume 1

Hekate

Edited by Vikki Bramshaw

PUBLISHED BY AVALONIA
WWW.AVALONIABOOKS.COM

PUBLISHED BY AVALONIA
BM AVALONIA
LONDON
WC1N 3XX
ENGLAND, UK

WWW.AVALONIABOOKS.COM

THE MANY GODS ANTHOLOGIES
VOLUME 1
HEKATE

COPYRIGHT © VARIOUS CONTRIBUTORS, AS CREDITED.

ISBN: 978-1-905297-33-7
(PAPERBACK)

FIRST EDITION, MAY 2024

COVER ART © LARRY PHILLIPS, 2014
ILLUSTRATIONS AND PHOTOGRAPHS AS CREDITED.

DESIGNED AND PRODUCED BY AVALONIA LTD
BM AVALONIA, LONDON, WC1N 3XX, UNITED KINGDOM
WWW.AVALONIABOOKS.COM

ALL RIGHTS RESERVED.

British Library Cataloguing in Publication Data. A catalogue record for this book is available from the British Library.

Every effort has been made to credit material to, and obtain permission from, copyright holders for the use of their work. If you notice any errors or omissions, please notify the publisher so that corrections can be incorporated into future editions of this work. The information provided in this book hopes to inspire and inform. The authors and publisher assume no responsibility for the effects, or lack thereof, obtained from the practices described in this book.

The reproduction of any part of this book, except for review purposes, is strictly prohibited in all formats without the prior written consent of Avalonia Ltd. and the copyright holders.

IN MEMORY OF
JAMES VAN KOLLENBURG

Kallímakhos
Founder of hellenicgods.org

Table of Contents

Foreword by Vikki Bramshaw _____ 9
Contributor Biographies _____ 13

Many-Named & Faced Goddess: An Introduction to Hekate & Household Devotion _____ 19
Mater Deum Magna Idaea: A Force of Heaven & Earth _____ 30
Iberia at the Crossroads _____ 44
Sacred Shakespeare: The creation of Hekate Genesis _____ 50
Entering the Temple of Medea: Hero Cult, Spiritual Ancestry & Hekatean Devotion _____ 62
Hekate & the Brazilian Crossroads _____ 71
Hecate's Dreams & Oracles _____ 80
The Lamia: Followers of Hekate _____ 90
Searching for Lamia _____ 101
The Ephesian Letters _____ 104
The Orphic Hymn to Hekate _____ 107
The Importance of the Orphic Hymn in Modern Practice _____ 112
Hekate in the Living Orphic Tradition _____ 127
Kore vs. Crone: History, Transcendence & Respect _____ 147
Hekate Rexchthon: Raising up the Goddess _____ 155
The Numbers of Hekate _____ 169

Index _____ 173

Foreword

VIKKI BRAMSHAW

'Askei Kataskei Eron Oreon Ior Mega Samnyer Baui ... Phobantia Semne!' - charm associated with initiation & the goddess Hekate (PGM LXX.12)

Welcome to the beginnings of *The Many Gods Anthologies*, a new series of publications bringing together scholarly papers and accounts of personal gnosis about the deities who hold a special place in our hearts. This is *Volume 1 – Hekate*.

It is probably true that several gods and goddesses have become particularly popular as part of the modern witchcraft movement and pagan reconstructionism. Several of these gods were brought to the forefront of the modern mind by the Romanticism of the 19th and early 20th centuries. Luminaries such as Keats and Wordsworth, Shelley and Kipling (enraptured by the Satyr God Pan) and early amateur anthropologists such as James Frazer, Robert Graves and Charles Leland, who idealised the religious practices of our ancestors, all contributed to this popularity. This was despite, in some cases, the dubious evidence.

Naturally, the presence of these divine names and concepts in the collective consciousness would influence the occult movement that would follow, with the likes of Aleister Crowley and the Golden Dawn utilising some of these deities within their own rites (in this case, often more as 'desirable qualities' or, influencing factors rather than gods to appease or supplicate; not a new concept, we see this approach in ancient magic too). It is so interesting how some of these gods have evolved; by the mid to late 20th century, writers such as Doreen Valiente and other contemporary authors had published works or promoted traditions which embraced these gods as central beings. The likes of Pan and Aradia, and even demi-gods and phantoms (such as Herne, the ghostly antlered figure of Windsor Forest) were being conflated with other more significant divinities and elevated to a more divine status. Whilst not all of our readers will identify with these specific written works and traditions, it cannot be denied that they had some hand in the resurgence, evolution, and elevation of these divine beings.

But aside from published works and occult traditions, the resurgence of certain old gods is part of what I understand as a much more fascinating global event. Whilst the names of those gods and spirits are indeed recognised and their stories embraced (by both ancient and modern culture), we see a more subtle reemergence of other facets of their nature and worship - and even other conflated deities that have made themselves known by way of association but also by way of the 'current'. This is the phenomenon of a 'wave' of interest in one specific topic or subject for no reason other than perhaps the planets were aligned so that a focus of interest begins to snowball. This is undoubtedly the case for such deities as the goddess Hekate, who has seen a significant rise in popularity since the early 2000s, and also the God Dionysos – both deities enjoying a huge wave of interest and publications and by association, the same can often be said for other deities who are associated or conflated with them.

So perhaps their elevation is partly driven by written works, but the reality of the esoteric current reaches beyond marketing or media. It is a current of energy, of occult knowledge and awareness, which lends itself to those who are open to its influence. It is something that moves apart from us, towards us, through us. Perhaps it is an unconscious response to the state of the world as a wider whole. Perhaps there are certain forces that we need right now in the present climate. Perhaps it is due to the power of repetition, a technique taught in the practice of magic. The repetition of a name, phrase or action reinforces that concept, idea, spirit or deity, or brings that requirement into being (and this is why it is argued that evoking a more 'popular' deity or spirit to aid our magic will be more successful than using a lesser-known one). Perhaps the energy itself is separate from the deity, yet driven by them, and influencing things on a wider scale; the microcosm influencing the macrocosm, akin to other forces and correspondences of the universe. Or perhaps it is a little of all of the above.

What follows in these pages is a selection of papers written from different perspectives about the goddess Hekate. It seemed appropriate to start the *Many Gods Anthologies* with the goddess Hekate, who has already undergone this wave of interest and whose worship has been firmly rekindled during the past few decades. What has been very clear is the amount of academic material supporting Hekate's history and worship and, by association, her rituals and magic. It is also appropriate to say that nothing is in isolation; like so many ancient Gods, the worship of Hekate and the use of her magic extends beyond the mortal boundaries of her native shores, with a wealth of academic research and archaeological evidence to support this.

I would like to extend my thanks to Sorita d'Este, the author of many published works on Hekate, for her hand in this project and, of course, as the Founder of the Covenant of Hekate, for her work in bringing the community together. I would also like to thank devotee Kenn Payne, for his contribution to this, both in its early days and ongoingly. Of course, a final thanks to all the wonderful contributors who have submitted their work and waited patiently for its publication.

Vikki Bramshaw (Editor) November 2023
New Forest, England

EDITORIAL NOTES

Hekate or Hecate?

The Greek transliteration of Hekate (with a 'k') and the Roman transliteration of Hecate (with a 'c') have been left unaltered reflecting the authors' preference in the essays. Both are taken to mean the same deity, who is the subject of this anthology.

Contributor Biographies

ARIADNE RAINBIRD (WALES, UK)

Ariadne Rainbird is a psychologist, priestess, druid, orphic, Wiccan and pagan chaplain living in the South Wales Valleys. Although she has studied many different paths over the years, she has always felt a pull towards Hellenic tradition and the Ancient Greek Gods, and over the past ten years or so she has dedicated herself to the Orphic path, within which Hekate has a very important role as Soteria, saviouress and advocate of the virtuous. Ariadne honours Hekate in the context of the Ancient Greek mystery traditions and has contributed to a number of devotional anthologies in honour of the Theoi.

B.P. SHOOP (NORTHERN VIRGINIA, USA)

Shoop is a Hellenic Polytheist, graduate student, and activist from Northern Virginia, USA. Shoop grew up in the Spiritualist church, which initially sparked their interest in magic, witchcraft, and the occult. They are a devotee of the goddess Hekate, who they've been honouring and studying for over a decade, as well as Medea and Kirke, Her priestesses. In addition, Shoop is working to become a historian focusing on LGBTQ+ social movements and politics in the 1970s. They balance this academic pursuit with their spiritual ones, studying Ancient Greek religious and magical practices in their spare time.

CARRIE KIRKPATRICK (LONDON, UK)

Carrie Kirkpatrick is an ordained Priestess of Hecate, a witch and psychic clairvoyant who has been guiding people psychically and magically for thirty-five years. She began working with the goddess in the 1990s and has worked extensively on TV and in the media as a producer and presenter, teaching people how to connect to goddess energies. She continues to work in television as a producer and director of factual programmes. Carrie founded Goddess Enchantment (Workshops & Training) in 2007, and regularly hosts experiential magical workshops with Caroline Wise exploring the goddesses. She is the author & photographer behind Goddess Enchantment (1&2) and the creator of the Goddess Enchantment Oracle (App). www.goddessenchantment.com

CHRISTINA MORAITI (ATHENS, GREECE)

Christina comes from a multicultural background, a polytheist since her teenage years and a devotee to the goddess Hekate. A lover of history, theurgy and witchcraft, Christina lives in Athens where her goal as a member of the Covenant of Hekate is the discovery and exploration of the Goddess' history and role throughout the centuries. A Keybearer of the Covenant, Christina feels her purpose is to explore Hekate's sacred epithets and find each and every depiction of her in museums and archaeological sites around the world, 'Following her Torches', all in harmony with the five principles of the Covenant. Contact: tita09@gmail.com.

EMILY CARDING (EAST SUSSEX, UK)

Emily Carding is a professional actor, writer and artist living by the sea in beautiful East Sussex. They are also the creator of The Transparent Tarot, The Transparent Oracle and The Tarot of the Sidhe for Schiffer Books and author of Faery Craft, So Potent Art: The Magic of Shakespeare and Seeking Faery with Llewellyn Publishing, as well as multiple essays for anthologies on various esoteric, mythical and mystical subjects. Emily holds a BA (hons) in Theatre Arts from Bretton Hall and an MFA in Staging Shakespeare from the University of Exeter. They have now appeared in versions of 24 of Shakespeare's plays on stage and screen and won multiple awards for their innovative approach to Shakespearean performance. They played a supporting role in the new Silent Hill film (2024). Emily is the co-creator of The Torchlit Path. www.emilycarding.com

FRANCINE DERSCHNER (SÃO PAOLO, BRAZIL)

Francine holds a Degree in History and has been fascinated by mythology and esotericism since she was a child. She began her journey in Wicca and, since then, found herself spiritually by rediscovering the Ancient Gods. She started her work with Hekate in 2012, when she was called to her service, and since then, she has integrally dedicated herself to the Goddess in her personal practices. As a Torchbearer of The Covenant of Hekate, Francine wants to assist the devotees in reconnection and rediscovery of the Goddess and light Hekate's sacred flames wherever she can.

HAZEL (LONDON, UK)

Hazel (pseudonym) is half Greek/half English, living in London. She discovered Hecate in her teens in Greece in the late 1990s, upon discovering her path with the Greek Gods. She joined the Covenant of Hekate in 2011, and is AIDA 2* qualified - and a mermaid! Being both a Torchbearer and Keybearer for the CoH, she advocates for the Oceanic/Einalian path, encouraging others to explore their emotional intelligence and learn more about Hecate Einalian and Krataiis.

JAMES VAN KOLLENBURG (KALLÍMAKHOS)

Throughout his adult life James explored a variety of religions. In his later years he became a Hellenist; worshipping the ancient gods of Greece and particularly identifying with Apollo. He became an expert in this area by reading and studying with Apollonia in Greece, who, over a number of years, taught him much about Hellenism and ancient Greece. He built an extensive library of Greek and Roman religion, art, philosophy, and language and furthered his education. He established hellenicgods.org, a site that grew into several hundred pages, and included text, images, and videos about Hellenism and ancient Greece. The site was frequented by scholars from all over the world, leading to lively discussions with scholars from large universities such as Harvard about his writings. James left this earthly plane on May 4, 2023.

LARRY PHILLIPS (U.S.A.)

Larry Phillips is an artist and magical practitioner living in eastern Kansas, U.S. He mainly uses oil paint as a medium and focuses on landscape and mythic subject matter, wherein Hekate is a frequent subject. His current system of magical practice synthesises his own occult history, including Wicca, ceremonial magic (Aurum Solis), traditional witchcraft, and chaos magic.

LYZA (UK)

Lyza (pseudonym) is a musician/dancer/educator/content creator currently living in her home county of Yorkshire, having previously lived in Wales and Oxford. Her practice has been based upon folk magick since her teens, with Hekate coming into her life at university and encouraging her to reach out to other Pagans in the area, which is how she met Hazel. She joined CoH in 2012 and finds Hekate Chthonia, Phosphoros and Geneteira to be the main faces of the goddess in her practice.

MARCEL SCHREI (GERMANY)

Marcel is a gay male witch from Germany. Influenced by a solitary wiccan-esque path, Zen Buddhism, Tarot and rugby, in combination with an urge to read everything he can, his goal is to learn as much about the divine and himself as possible. When trying to inspire others, Marcel emphasises the importance of respect and each individual's approach towards the divine, religion and magic.

NESS BOSCH (SCOTLAND, UK)

Ness is an Iberian Priestess and shamaness, author, researcher and teacher. She is the head of the Covenant of the Waters, the Goddess Temple Alba and the Temple of Astarte. She has walked an Animistic path for years. She travels internationally sharing her knowledge and experiences on the Path of Bones. Ness is the author of 'Sacred Bones, Magic Bones'. She lives in Scotland with her 3 children, from where she works as a Pagan Celebrant and holds space and activities for the pagan community in addition to training events and workshops. See www.nessbosch.com and www.thepathofthebones.com

ORRYELLE DEFENESTRATE-BASCULE (BELGIUM)

Orryelle Defenestrate-Bascule is an esoteric artist living in Belgium using many media including painting, writing, sculpture, sound, film and performance art. He is the Writer-Director of Australian-originating 'Metamorphic Ritual Theatre Company', who have presented many major original productions based on (and updating/mutating) various ancient mythos. Orryelle is the Author-Artist of 'Esezezus', a book on and of the Magic of Language (Grayle Press 2023) with accompanying album, 'The Tela Quadrivium' book-web from Fulgar Press (Conjunctio 2008, Coagula 2009, Solve 2012, Distillatio 2015) 'Time, Fate and Spider Magic' (Avalonia, 2014) and 'The Book of Kaos Tarot' (iNSPiRALink. Multimedia Press 2003). Orryelle is currently creating an esoteric sculpture garden in the Ardennes, where, in the meantime, he has a small Sabbat Gathering and interactive labyrinths.

SORITA D'ESTE (SOMERSET, UK)

Sorita is a priestess, author and adventurer who has been exploring the liminal worlds of magic, mysticism and religion since childhood. The author of more than a dozen books, including *Circle for Hekate, Artemis, Hekate Liminal Rites, Practical Elemental Magick* and *The Cosmic Shekinah*, her current projects include further work on Hekate, Artemis and the Goddess Diana. Sorita is the founder of Avalonia, an independent esoteric publisher, as well as the Covenant of Hekate in 2010. She facilitates ceremonies and workshops online and around the world. See www.soritadeste.com and www.theurgia-events.com

VIKKI BRAMSHAW (HAMPSHIRE, UK)

Vikki Bramshaw is an author and researcher committed to studying folklore, religious history, and the esoteric since the late 90s. Vikki has been involved in the Covenant of Hekate from its inception and contributed to the anthology 'Hekate: Her Sacred Fires' published in 2010. She then contributed essays to several anthologies, including 'VS: Duality and Conflict in Magick, Mythology and Paganism' before releasing the groundbreaking 'Dionysos: Exciter to Frenzy' in 2013, which explored the Greek God Dionysos and the extent of his influence on the ancient world. Most recently, Vikki's latest book, 'New Forest Folklore, Traditions & Charms' is a unique study taking a deeper look at the folklore and traditions of the ancient landscape of her native New Forest. Following this publication, she has assisted in curating museum exhibitions, and her research has been integrated into artists' projects. Vikki lives in the rural New Forest with her young son, hens, horses and one spirit cat.

See www.vikkibramshaw.co.uk

Shrine of the Sanctuary of Hekate Soteira, Glastonbury. The central statue of Hekate Phosphorous was made by Colin Irving (UK). The metal etching on the left is by Georgi Mishev, and the triple image on the right is by Grai Matter.

Many-Named & Faced Goddess:
An Introduction to Hekate & Household Devotion

Contributed by Sorita d'Este, Glastonbury, UK

Where do I start an introduction to the Goddess of many names and faces? A Goddess who is a protector, saviour, guide, and companion? A Goddess who cares for the young and who has a role in guiding the restless dead? Or perhaps, the Goddess of witchcraft and sorcery, who was honoured by Medea – arguably the most famous magical enchantress of all time?

I have dedicated more than two decades to researching and learning about Hekate. I spend a lot of time reading academic works and other literature, as well as listening to experiences modern-day devotees and practitioners of magic have with Her today. I have also been privileged to make pilgrimages to dozens of museums to see many of the ancient icons of the Goddess for myself. I have visited archaeological sites and their landscapes to imagine what life might have been like for those who knew Her name in ancient times and find context for the evidence they left behind. I have also visited modern temples, sanctuaries, and shrines that devotees in the here and now are creating for Her and spoken to others who are developing or hoping to create such spaces for Her. And all of this has taught me one thing – *There is always more to learn!*

This brief introduction to Hekate is intended to provide you with enough information about this primordial Goddess to be able to give context to the essays that follow. It is impossible to provide an introduction like this without repeating information that almost all devotees and practitioners who call on Hekate will already be familiar with, so I have done my best to blend the very well-known with some of the less discussed attributes of this primordial Goddess, so hopefully there is something for everyone! I also provide a simple introduction to household (or private) devotion for readers interested in exploring or deepening their relationship with Hekate. Deities - including Hekate - were celebrated publicly and privately in ancient times. Private celebrations were simple and often daily affairs. In contrast, the public or civic celebrations varied from simple community celebrations to large and elaborate state festivals, complete with games, entertainment and feasts and were less frequent.

HER NAME

The name *Hekate* is a transliteration from the Greek Ἑκατη; or *Hecate* based on the Latin. I favour *Hekate*, but both are correct and continue to be used interchangeably. Debate about the exact origins of her name continues, but *Hekate* is likely a female version of the name *Hekatos*, which is an epithet given to the god Apollo and can be translated as *far-shooter*.

In common with most of the deities of her time, cultic double names were often used for Hekate. This is where her name was combined with an epithet, creating a double-barrelled name. These usually originate from one of the following circumstances:

- Syncretisation with another deity, for example, *Artemis-Hekate or Isis-Hekate*.
- A specific cult role held by the deity, for example, *Hekate Kourotrophos* (Hekate child's nurse).
- Honorific titles given because of something the deity did. For example, *Hekate Soteira* (Hekate the Saviour) where she is given credit for safeguarding a place.
- Epithets can be descriptive, recording something of the appearance of the deity. For example, *Hekate Phosphoros* (*Hekate bearer of light*).

- Epithets may indicate a link to a particular location. Such as *Hekate Propylaia* (*Hekate by the gate*).
- *Polyonymy* is the use of many names for the same deity with the belief that they are all the same. This might also include the practice of interpretatio Romano or interpretatio Graeca, where the names of deities were translated into that of the names of the new culture or empire. So, for example, Hekate is sometimes translated as *Diana* – with both deities being *Trivia* (*of the three ways*) when she is included in the Roman pantheon.

HEKATE IN EARLY LITERATURE

Hekate is named as early as the mid-7th century BCE by Hesiod in his *Theogony*, where she is given a unique and almost exalted place. This has led to speculation that Hesiod may have been a devotee of Hekate (as he was born in Anatolia) or that perhaps the initiatory mysteries of the Orphic tradition influenced the text[1]. In my opinion none of this diminishes or negates the importance of the text.

A few decades after Hesiod's work, we find Hekate in the story told in Homer's *Hymn to Demeter* – the story at the centre of the famous Eleusinian Mysteries that tells the story of Demeter and her daughter Persephone. In it, Hekate first takes on the role of guide and helper to Demeter, taking her to speak to the Sun God Helios, and then becomes the yearly companion and guide to Persephone on her annual journey to and from Hades. Hekate is frequently depicted with Persephone and Demeter, often as a trio.

By the 4th century BCE, we find a reference in the writings of Pausanias, the ancient Greek travel writer, who wrote of a triple statue of the Goddess in Athens:

---

[1] See Hekate in the Living Orphic Tradition by Rainbird, chapter 11.

> *"It was Alcamenes, in my opinion, who first made three images of Hecate attached to one another, a figure called by the Athenians Epipurgidia (on the Tower); it stands beside the temple of the Wingless Victory..."*[2]

ORIGINS

There is a fascination with looking at the past for clues about the deities or practices we value. I believe this fascination is driven by a primordial desire to connect to the origin of our story, driven by a quest for tradition and rites of passage— which is increasingly rare in Western culture. History is essential because it connects us to our origins and our ancestors. By incorporating the myths, lessons and wisdom we learn from the past into our present, we enable ourselves to create a diverse but solid foundation for the future. A foundation rooted in the past but standing firm in the present day.

So, where did Hekate come from? The oldest known icon attributed to Hekate, showing her single-bodied and enthroned, dates to the 6th century BCE and was found in Athens (Greece). Some claim that a triple terracotta image of Hekate found at Selinunte, Sicily dating to the 5th century, is the oldest. The oldest known sanctuary inscription dates to the 6th century BCE and was found at the archaeological site of Miletus (Türkiye). This was a few decades after Hesiod's Theogony, but of course, the worship of this Goddess would have been well established by this time.

Hekate likely evolved out of earlier cults in Anatolia (modern Türkiye), perhaps the Caria region, where one can still visit the remains of her late Hellenic temple at Lagina. In this region, many names seem to be derived from the same root as *Hekate* and *Hekatos,* which can be seen as evidence of her possible popularity in the region[3].

---

[2] Description of Greece, Pausanias, 2nd century CE, trans. Jones, 1918.
[3] See for example the Hecatomnids, a ruling dynasty in the region.

Examining Hekate's symbols and other attributes, it is easy to make connections to goddesses with much older established cults and a much wider geographical region. For example, we find intriguing clues linking Hekate to earlier goddesses from Anatolia and Persia, Phoenicia (Canaan), Thrace, the Levant, Mesopotamia, Greece and Rome. In polytheistic cultures, deities were customarily adopted, adapted, and sometimes translated or equated to the gods of other cultures or tribes. These regions were places of culture and trade, which was possible because of the movement of people and goods – and with that, continuous exchanges of ideas and knowledge, including information about the gods and their worship. Based on the evidence we have available today, Hekate likely evolved from an earlier cult of the *Magna Mater (The Great Mother)* in Asia Minor. Ideas and practices from further afield were assimilated into her worship over centuries, together with epithets and symbols.

Portion of the frieze from the Temple of Hekate, Lagina. It is on display in the Museum of Archaeology in Istanbul, Turkiye. Photo © d'Este, 2022

WHAT IS HEKATE A GODDESS OF?

Hekate held many roles over the centuries; today, modern-day devotees continue to attribute new roles to her. In the 20th century, Hekate's role as a goddess of witchcraft and magic and her association with the restless dead was emphasised in many of the roles she was given as part of the magical and Pagan revivals. She was also given the dubious role of *Crone* in a *Maiden Mother Crone* triplicity construct, which evolved during the 20th century and gained popularity sometime during the 1970s. Deities do take on new names, mantles, and symbols over time, but when it comes to gods who are ancient and immortal, concepts of human ageing, let alone trying to force a goddess into new shapes, would seem foolish, redundant and irrelevant.

Some of Hekate's popular roles include:
- Agricultural (associated with the grain mysteries of Demeter and when worshipped with Hermes livestock will increase);
- Child's Nurse (a wet nurse for the young);
- Dreams (said to be able to send nightmares, but also invoked for Dream Oracles to gain insight);
- Magic & Sorcery (numerous examples of spells, curse tablets and charms have been found, and these practices continue in her name today);
- Oracles (Oracles of prophecy, as well as the Chaldean Oracles);
- Plants & Herbs (knowledge of their use);
- Protector (at gateways, thresholds, for individuals & cities);
- Sovereignty (she decides the outcome of battles);
- The Mysteries (she holds an essential role in the Mysteries at Eleusis, Aegina, Samothrace and elsewhere;
- The Restless Dead (those who die before their time might join Hekate's retinue);
- Travel (protects travellers).

HEKATE'S SYMBOLS

The ancient images of the Gods provide clues about their nature, roles and powers. The objects they are shown with, how they are dressed, and the beings depicted with them are part of a symbolic language through which knowledge is passed down. This language is also what we use to pray and invoke our deities. Successful ritual combines symbols, language and material objects to attract the deity to us. It takes knowledge, experience and intuition to successfully combine these in a ritual.

Following is a list of symbols[4] associated with the goddess Hekate, which, when seen in combination, usually indicates that the image or icon of a deity we are looking at or reading about is the Goddess Hekate. Most of these symbols are also associated with other deities, so to avoid confusion, it is helpful to learn more about their contextual use and meaning.

- Brazen Sandals
- Bulls & Cows
- Daggers or Swords
- Dogs
- Horses
- Light (including lamps)
- Modius (a headdress worn by Hekate, Demeter and others)
- Moon
- Pillars & Trees (esp. the Oak tree)
- Polos (a headdress worn by Hekate)
- Rays of Light
- Snakes
- Stags (Deer)
- Stars
- Torches (usually two, but can be one or up to six!)
- Veil (indicating an association with the Moon or Oracles)
- Whips

PRIVATE OR "HOUSEHOLD" DEVOTION

Private devotion and offerings given to Hekate would have been similar to that given to most of the gods in an ancient

---

[4] Discussed in more detail in Circle for Hekate, 2017 (volume 1)

household. Worship would have taken place at a shrine in the home where all the Gods worshipped by the household would have representations or at an altar in the garden or courtyard of the property – with additional observances on special days.

Today, like in the past, household shrines are best placed somewhere private and continue to be spaces where devotion and offerings are made. For Hekate you could also have a shrine in the porch or gateway of your home, as was done in ancient Athens honouring Hekate as the guardian on the threshold, protectress of your home.

Household devotion does not need to be complicated, and providing it is done with respect, there are no absolute rights or wrongs. Your shrine can be as small or large as your circumstances allow. Likewise, for offerings, you could research historical offerings, or you could instead offer local and seasonal produce.

HEKATE SUPPERS

The Hekate Supper or deipna is perhaps the most talked about historical ritual offered to Hekate, even though remarkably little information about it survives from the ancient world.

Johnston wrote that:

> *"Plutarch says that these suppers were intended for Hekate and also for... the gods who averted evil."* [5]

Aristophanes' words provide us with the source of the ideas that are most often repeated. Plutus was first produced in 388 BCE as a satire on the politics of Athens at the time, and in it there is a reference to the suppers, saying:

> *"Ask Hekate whether it is better to be rich or starving; she will tell you that the rich send her a meal every month and that the poor make it disappear before it is even served."* [6]

---

[5] Crossroads, Johnston, 1991.
[6] Plutus, Aristophanes, 380 BCE, trans. anon.

The idea that people experiencing poverty took the food resonates with many modern practitioners, who no longer leave food at the crossroads but instead donate food (or money) to shelters and food banks. This is an option, but it is worth remembering that the crossroads rituals of history were more than acts of charity; they were done for purification and protection.

In most parts of the world today, it would be unusual for food left at crossroads to be taken by those in need; it is more than likely to be eaten by local wildlife instead. If you decide to leave food at a crossroads, adapt the food and offering vessels to suit the circumstances, and ensure that you do not leave litter or food that is harmful to the wildlife where you are.

SHRINE

The first step for household devotion is to create your shrine. You can be creative with this and adapt it to your circumstances, make it big, small, inside or outside – but make it the best you can make it.

- An icon or representation of the Goddess (this is optional but nice).
- Cloth – to use as a covering for the shrine. My personal preference is white or red for Hekate.
- Fire: A lamp [7] or a candlestick with a candle [8].
- Incense: A censer or fireproof container, charcoal and incense grains – alternatively, use incense sticks. [9]

---

[7] If using an oil lamp, use natural products only such as olive oil, rather than chemical oil products – remember it is an offering! If using candles, it is best to obtain a good quality pillar style candle with a long burning time, again take care to select a candle made from natural products if possible.

[8] Always take safety precautions and ensure that you never leave any flames unattended.

[9] Take care to buy natural incense grains and incense sticks made from quality natural materials – remember this is an offering!

- Libations: You will need a bowl or other container for food and liquid offerings. The container should be used only for offerings, not for other purposes.
- Offerings: A selection of vessels (bowls, vases, jugs and baskets) to place offerings into in preparation for libation.
- Basin: a large bowl for you to wash your hands in, which will be used for ritual cleansing[10].
- A larger box or basket to store your items in when not used.

DEVOTIONAL RITUAL (EXAMPLE)

Today, household devotion continues to be very individual, but here is an example of a format you can adapt to your own preferences and circumstances:

- Ritual cleansing: Wash your hands and enter the space where your shrine is in quiet contemplation, reflecting on your reasons for wishing to offer devotion..
- Light your fire.
- Offer a hymn or song to the Goddess.[11]
- Make libations or food offerings, if appropriate.
- Give thanks to the Goddess in your own words..
- Extinguish your flame.

You will need to dispose of the offerings you poured or placed into your libation bowl, which can be challenging for those living in large modern cities. It is, however, important that offerings are never disposed of as rubbish, and instead that you make time to take it somewhere, where you can respectfully offer it to the earth. If disposal is difficult, adapt your offerings to suit your situation. You could, for example, offer your work, creativity or time in

---

[10] It is nice to have a dedicated basin for this use, but if you are short on space, you can do your purifications in your bathroom sink!
[11] For example, the Orphic Hymn to Hekate – translations offered in essays in this volume by Christina Moraiti and James van Killenburg (Kallimakhos).

service to an appropriate community or cause, or you could change the offerings to something that does not need disposal often, such as burning oil in a lamp or offering water as in small, poured libations into a pot plant you grow as part of a shrine.

I will leave you with the opening words of an essay I wrote for the Hekate: Her Sacred Fires anthology (2010), as it is as true now as it was then:

> *"Hekate is a Goddess of great antiquity. She is primordial, powerful and sometimes animalistic - and yet also sophisticated, modern and capable of adapting to different cultures. She is the Torchbearer, the Cosmic World Soul, the Guide and Companion. She is Mistress of the Restless Dead, who rules over the Heavens, Earth and Sea. She is the Keybearer who stands at the crossroads of life, death and initiation. Her devotees today, as throughout the ages, include philosophers, poets, sorcerers, theurgists, witches, root-cutters, enchantresses and ordinary people.*
> *She has been loved, feared and hated throughout the millennia of her known history. Depicted variously as three-formed facing in three directions, as well as sometimes with the heads of animals – and at other times as single-bodied standing bearing torches, or enthroned like the depictions of the goddess Kybele, Hekate has and possibly will always remain one of the greatest enigmas amongst the gods.*
> *It is easy to believe that, like many of the other gods, her mysteries were forgotten, only to re-emerge and be reconstructed at the hands of the modern Pagan revival, but even just scratching at the surface of the available evidence soon provides us with a different story. She was never forgotten, and maybe just maybe, there has never been a time in which fires weren't kept burning for her somewhere, nor a time in which offerings were not made in her name."*

Further learning & resources:

Circle for Hekate, 2017 – Sorita d'Este
Hekate Liminal Rites, 2009 – d'Este & Rankine
Hellenic Polytheism: Household Worship, 2014 – Labrys
The Covenant of Hekate – www.hekatecovenant.com
Meeting in the Circle – www.theurgia-events.com

Mater Deum Magna Idaea:
A Force of Heaven & Earth

Contributed by Vikki Bramshaw, The New Forest, UK

Hekate assumed a number of titles during antiquity, but one often overlooked is that of a mother goddess. Historical texts such as the *Greek Magical Papyri*, the *Chaldean Oracles* and Proclus' *Hymn to Hekate* all refer to Hekate as a mother goddess; she is hailed as the 'Mother of Gods'[12] and conflated with deities such as the Greek Rhea. This is of course in conflict with the impression of Hekate given by the likes of Aleister Crowley in the early 1900s, who described Hekate as a *'woman past all hope of motherhood'*[13] a remodelling of Hekate in the modern consciousness which may be responsible for her contemporary identification as a crone. It is true that the legends of Hekate do not describe her as a mother in the conventional sense; at least, not a literal one. She is sometimes referred to as *Kourotrophos* (child-nourisher) and *Episkopos* (overseer) and the epithet *Enodia* can indicate an involvement in the protection of children[14] but very rarely is Hekate portrayed as a mother herself. Certainly, she is the spiritual mother of her priestesses Medea and Circe and otherworldly creatures such as the *Lamia* and the *Scylla*, but her role as a mother goddess is more indicative o

f her position as psychopomp between the worlds, of transition, the birth of the cosmos and her role as protector. In the *Chaldean Oracles* Hekate is referred to as the source of all

---

[12] Prayer to Selene for Any Spell, The Greek Magical Papyri
[13] Alistair Crowley, Moonchild 1929
[14] Christopher A. Faraone, The Transformation of Greek Amulets

things, the *World Soul* - but again, this role is a spiritual and/or metaphorical one of transformation and liminal spaces.

It is thought that the earliest account of Hekate, a passage in the *Theogony*, gives us some clues about the nature of her original Anatolian form. In this account, Hekate is described as a significant and most elevated goddess who was 'gifted with portions of the earth and sea' and *'honoured exceedingly by the deathless gods'*.[15] She is further described as a goddess to petition for a favourable outcome on the battleground, whilst also worshipped by sheep farmers as she is able to both *'increase* (the flock) *from a few, or make many* (sheep) *to be less'*.[16] This passage offers evidence that the cult of Hekate existed in Hesiod's time (circa 700 BCE) and describes the sort of goddess she was; a dominant goddess with the power to deliver, but also to destroy. At this point, let's rewind over 8000 years of history back to the Neolithic city of Çatalhöyük.

In the ancient city of Çatalhöyük (southern Anatolia/modern-day Türkiye) a 6000 BCE figurine was found. Seated between two lions or leopards and with bull horns at her feet, scholars described her as a voluptuous mother-goddess figure, portrayed as if giving birth; yet, the classification of a mother goddess is open to interpretation. It can be argued that our general understanding of a 'mother goddess' is largely influenced by the likes of 19th and early 20th-century amateur anthropologists, who made assumptions based on the status quo (largely, the idea that a 'fertility goddess' was at the source of all early religion). In fact, the latest research suggests that this icon (and others similar to it) may depict a throned figure of importance or even royalty - not necessarily a literal mother, but the Mother of the State[17] which wouldn't be such a stretch of the imagination given that the 'mother' role is not always a physical one, but a metaphorical one.

---

[15] Theogony (411-52)
[16] Theogony (411-52)
[17] Birgitte Bøgh, The Phrygian Background of Kybele

She is the overseer of all things, *'Ephoros'* and mediator. Other figurines of the same goddess at Çatalhöyük showed further insight; a female icon with a 'robust' body on one side and a skeleton on the other.[18] Several of these goddess-forms had been placed at household shrines (NB, it is interesting to note that Hekate was also worshipped at household shrines rather than official temples) and over the bones of the dead, who were buried under the floor. In this juxtaposed position, the Çatalhöyük goddess is the ultimate psychopomp between the worlds; she symbolises the transition between birth and death, the living and the dead. Here we find the same ideas conveyed in the *Theogony;* a life-giving goddess who gives birth to the very beasts whom she later sacrifices, she giveth and she taketh away.

Archaeologists suggest that the iconography of the Çatalhöyük goddess points to the Anatolian/ Phrygian Kybele[19] the *Mater Deum Magna Idaea*, 'Great Idaean Mother of the Gods'[20] ('Mater' being the Greek for the Phrygian *Matar*, for 'Mother').[21] It is believed that Kybele originated as the land spirit *Kubileya*, a name derived from a Phrygian word for 'mountain,' leading to her appellation as 'Mother of the Mountain'. It is also interesting that *Hesychios*, writing much later in circa in 5th century AD, described Kybele as a literal topographical feature of the landscape, *'the mountains of Phrygia, and caves and hollow places,'* - an animist statement. The presence of enshrined human bones at Çatalhöyük points also to Kybele's entanglement with the idea of death and perhaps, ancestral veneration. We find evidence that the dead had first been set out for scavenging birds before reaching their resting place[22]-sensible for a goddess of the mountains who was often depicted with birds of prey whose figurine was accompanied by bird bones and feathers. We find

---

[18] L Meskell & C Nakamura, Çatalhöyük 2005 Archive Report – Figurines
[19] Walter Burkert, Homo Necans 1972
[20] Encyclopaedia Britannica
[21] Birgitte Bøgh, The Phrygian Background of Kybele
[22] Walter Burkert, Homo Necans 1972

that after defleshing, the bones of the body would be painted with bright colours such as red, green, and blue before being buried, and at times, later dug back up for ritualistic activities. (NB, Kybele's association with birds of prey and bird bones opens up a whole new conversation on the ritual intentions of Çatalhöyük - the birds, some scholars suggest, acted as mediators between this world and the spirit world.)[23]

Kybele was also considered a protective spirit of the home and identified with the *Agathae Tyche*, a feminine primitive spirit of Greek folklore and magic.[24] In this role, she was held as the city protector, guardian of entrances and thresholds; faux doorways were carved into the rock of the early mountainsides sacred to Kybele and in later reliefs, she is depicted standing at doorways. Additionally, her cult locations were often found at crossroads, city gates and boundaries such as the edge of the city[25] all strikingly similar to the iconography surrounding Hekate. Kybele would become widespread across the Greek colonies during the Archaic period where she would influence Greek culture and eventually become identified with the 'Mother of Gods' Rhea (and several other deities) from at least the mid-6th century. So, it appears that the Great Mother was far from a simple goddess of fertility; in fact, the researcher Birgette Bøgh writes that there the absence of fertility symbols is noticeable, and that very few Matar statues show her with children - with even the best example not proven beyond doubt to be Matar.[26]

The name *Hekate* itself remains obscure but is probably of Anatolian origin.[27] The connections between Kybele and Hekate are numerous, with her position at her major cult centre of the Temple of Hekate at Lagina (western Anatolia, modern-day

---

[23] Nerissa Russell, Spirit Birds at Neolithic Çatalhöyük
[24] John Ferguson, The Religions of the Roman Empire
[25] Birgitte Bøgh, The Phrygian Background of Kybele
[26] Birgitte Bøgh, The Phrygian Background of Kybele
[27] Mihai Remus Feraru, The Cult of the Goddess Hekate in Miletus - Ziridava Studia Archaelogica 35

Türkiye) unrivalled.[28] These similarities include some important pieces of iconography such as their triple-form, dogs, keys, serpents, torches and enthronement (NB, we find the earliest example of Hekate seated in the 'Kybele pose' from Athens dated around.600 BCE, later throned and flanked by lions 400 BCE).[29] Kybele and Hekate also shared associations with other deities, such as Artemis who would be conflated with Hekate by the 5th BCE. Whilst researchers favour Anatolia as the root origin for Hekate, it is also likely that some form of Hekate was already established in Greece; with the decipherment of the Linear B tablets came the important discovery that many of the deities of classical Greece could be traced back to the Bronze Age on the Greek mainland, including Hekate.[30] For instance, one inscription found in Pylos, dated circa 1200 BCE, listed a number of early goddess names which included a deity named *Ipemedeja*. In later Greek mythology, Ipemedeja (or *Iphimede*) was an attendant of Artemis and given the epithet *'in the road'* an appellation usually applied to Hekate. Perhaps it is more likely that Ipemedeja literally meant *Hekate 'in the road'* i.e. an older Greek form of Hekate.[31]

So, whilst Kybele and Hekate are likely to have had independent roots, they are closely connected and were almost certainly conflated and synchronised. The Greek Hekate would have been exposed to the Anatolian influences encountered at cult centres such as Lagina, whilst Greek writers such as Hesiod would have interpreted Anatolian culture with their own ideas and the status quo of their time - including political agendas. It is important to consider the factors involved in the transmission of deities. For instance, Kybele became elevated in Rome in 204 BCE when, following a prophecy given in the *Sibylline Books*, the Romans introduced the cult of Kybele to help conquer their enemies. This is unlikely to have been an accidental happening

---

[28] William Berg, Hecate: Greek or Anatolian? Numen Vol. XXI
[29] Sorita d'Este, Historical Origins: Her Sacred Fires
[30] William Berg, Hecate: Greek or Anatolian? Numen Vol. XXI
[31] William Berg, Hecate: Greek or Anatolian? Numen Vol. XXI

and would have almost certainly had some political force behind it. But consequently, the cult of Kybele quickly became one of the most prominent cults in the Roman world.[32] Either way, Kybele and Hekate were firmly identified and/or conflated by the 3rd BCE.[33]

> *'Hekate, when invoked by the names of a bull, a dog and a lioness, is more propitious.'[34]*

As mistress of all domains, Kybele was not only the mother of gods and mountains but also of humans and beasts;[35] (NB, it's relevant to mention that the Minoan Mistress of Animals, *Potna Theron*, c.1500 BCE, was in turn identified with Kybele.)[36] An icon shared by both Hekate and Kybele was the lion or leopard, with both deities shown in the company of big cats. Certainly, both lions and leopards were once found native to Anatolia and would have been a feature of the Anatolian landscape. Depictions of Kybele throughout the Greco-Roman period would show her flanked by lions, using lions as footstools, in the company of lions protecting tombs, riding lion-drawn chariots, and even with lions resting their paws upon her head. Sometimes, Kybele would be accompanied by Hekate in her lion-drawn chariot, emphasising the connection between these deities.[37] In her traditional Çatalhöyük pose, Kybele is found seated with her hands upon the heads of lions, demonstrating power, control and authority over the natural world; later, she would even be described as *'lion-breeding'* suggesting a physical embodiment as a lioness.[38] About 200 miles from Çatalhöyük is the underrated archaeological site *Hacilar*, where we find images of enthroned goddess-figures cradling felines to their chests and pregnant women decorated in

---

[32] Encyclopedia Britannica
[33] Sorita d'Este, Historical Origins: Her Sacred Fires
[34] Porphyry, On Abstinence
[35] Encyclopedia Britannica
[36] Sorita d'Este, Historical Origins: Her Sacred Fires
[37] Sorita d'Este, Historical Origins: Her Sacred Fires
[38] Nonnus, Dionysiaca c.500CE

leopard patterns, positioned in feline poses.[39] In command of lions and leopards, Kybele was symbolic of power and domination and more anciently, the governess of the hunt. Wall murals at Çatalhöyük show masked 'leopard men' wearing leopard and deer skins, hunting deer and cattle, and performing dance or ritual in an example of magical appropriation.[40] We also find figurines of men riding leopards. (NB, in later Greek art, we find men in masks disguised as prey being attacked by leopards,[41] it is interesting to note the global phenomenon of the hunter becoming the hunted which would be reflected in future mystery cults, during which feasting often followed a death and 'ritual killing' made part of the feast).[42]

If as a lion he shake his bristling mane, I will cry "Euoi!" to Bacchos (Dionysos) on the arm of buxom Rhea (Kybele) stealthily draining the breast of the lionbreeding goddess.[43]

As Kybele was a goddess of mountain ranges, so Dionysos was the god of mountains, and Kybele was frequently associated and worshipped together with him (albeit sometimes with different Dionysian appellations, such as *Zagreus*, *Attis* and *Iacchos*). Indeed, in her later incarnation as Rhea, Kybele was referred to as the mother and teacher of Dionysos[44] and she cared for him inside a mountainside cavern, recalling earlier legends that described Dionysos' association with honey, mead, and its fermentation inside caves. (NB, see *'Dionysos Exciter to Frenzy'* for more on this topic). Wearing leopard skins about their shoulders, the *Maenads*, the priestesses of Dionysos, were known to spring up the hillsides with ease like leopards where they would shapeshift and allegedly, tear at raw flesh with their teeth. In this condition, the Maenads were looked upon as predatory beasts

---

[39] Lynn E Roller, In Search of God the Mother: The Cult of Anatolian Cybele
[40] Vikki Bramshaw, Dionysos: Exciter to Frenzy
[41] Walter Burkert, Homo Necans 1972
[42] Walter Burkert, Homo Necans 1972
[43] Nonnus, Dionysiaca c.500CE
[44] Nonnus, Dionysiaca c.500CE

themselves[45] and Euripides writes that the women *'changed into panthers'*[46] while Kybele's *Korybantes* were wild-natured spirits, indulging in animalistic dance, music and seductive rites.[47]

> *'...the night-wandering Zagreus (Dionysos) and the raw flesh-eating feasts ... the torches of the Mountain Mother (Kybele) Bakchos (Dionysos) of the Korybantes I invoked.'*[48]

The Orphic Hymns named big cats figuratively as *'Bull Slayers'*. At Çatalhöyük we find a bull cult (with striking similarities to the Bull Cult of Minoan Crete, where the cult of Kybele was absorbed into that of Rhea) and depictions of the goddess surrounded by bull horns, which in some cases appear to emerge from between her thighs;[49] the implication being that she will birth a bull in a chthonic paradox of life and death. (NB, this is of course, echoed in the later tales of the Minotaur, the love-child of Pasiphae the wife of King Minos and a sacred white bull). Here too, we find metaphorical or mythical motherhood - the birth of a beast or an anthropomorphic god, rather than a literal child. But significantly, Kybele is also one of the first goddesses consorting with the Horned God in his most ancient form, the bull-faced *Sabazios* of Anatolian ecstatic ritual[50] a cult in which Dionysos finds so many of his roots as Lord of Wild Beasts. The sacrifice of a bull was seen as a symbol of transition between this world and the next and in *The Odyssey*, the blood of cattle was used by Odysseus to open a gateway to the underworld, a powerful medium to travel between the realms.[51] Preparation of the sacrificial bull in ancient Greece included its bathing and decoration, with wreaths hung around its neck and its horns painted with gold. Burkert writes that the sacrificial animal was then sprinkled with water to get it to shake, *'imitating a 'willing nod' or perhaps the shuddering of the*

---

[45] Vikki Bramshaw, Dionysos: Exciter to Frenzy
[46] Euripides, The Bacchae
[47] Lynn E Roller, In Search of God the Mother: The Cult of Anatolian Cybele
[48] Porphyry, Kretes
[49] Walter Burkert, Homo Necans 1972
[50] Vikki Bramshaw, Dionysos: Exciter to Frenzy
[51] Homer, The Odyssey

Pythia',⁵² the oracular Priestesses of Delphi, before the sacrifice; the blood was then collected. A ritual held in tribute to Magna Mater in Rome, the *Taurobolium*, involved bathing in the blood of the sacred bull, but may have originated in some earlier form in Anatolia in honour of Kybele and Dionysos.⁵³ As a side note, Kybele and Hekate's more ancient Anatolian associations with dairy animals (both as nurturer and slaughterer) may indicate their connection with meat, milk and cheeses (or abstinence from it) an ongoing theme of their mystery cults. Hekate (and other deities identified with her) favoured offerings of milk and honey, with *meilikratos* prescribed as a magic drink in the *Greek Magical Papyri* (see PGM I. 1-42 and 262-347) in fact, the undertaking of its preparation was considered a spell or offering in itself. Dionysos was also associated with *meilikratos*: a mixture of honey and milk, two of the most primal foods.

Hekate was sometimes called upon as part of sacrificial magic and this may be linked with the common ground she holds with Kybele, whose cult in later incarnations required exceptional sacrifice such as bloody self-castration (of the *Castratos* or *Gallos*) and ritual bloodletting.⁵⁴ Perhaps, this is partly why both Hekate and Kybele shared the epithet *Brimo*, 'the terrifying'. It is also relevant at this point to mention Artemis again, a goddess who was incredibly fond of bloody sacrifice and whom we have already identified was conflated with Hekate in magic (NB: although, there are many fewer examples of blood sacrifice associated with Hekate than Artemis, who was regularly offered animals on a huge scale). Like Hekate, a significant influence on Artemis' cult and worship lies in Kybele. Kybele was worshipped at Ephesus by the 10ᵗʰ century BCE and was probably the precursor to Artemis who would come to preside over Ephesus.⁵⁵ At Samothrace too, the consort of Dionysos was known as

---

⁵² Walter Burkert, Homo Necans 1972
⁵³ Vikki Bramshaw, Dionysos: Exciter to Frenzy
⁵⁴ Birgitte Bøgh, The Phrygian Background of Kybele
⁵⁵ Sorita d'Este, Historical Origins: Her Sacred Fires

Axiokerse, *'worthy horned goddess'* who was likely to have been another early guise of Artemis and was also fond of bloodletting.[56] Incidentally, Dionysos was also conflated with Apollo (who usurped Dionysos, the original deity presiding over such places as the Oracular Sanctuary of Delphi)[57] and we find in PGM II 'Magical Handbook' (1-64) a blood sacrifice to *Apollo Paian*, which involves using the brain of a black ram and an ibis as part of the operation - indicating that this practice of bloody sacrifice even reached the reams of the more 'proper' Apollonian magic.

Another interesting piece of sacrificial spellwork is from the PGM III 'Magical Handbook' (1-164) *'Cat Ritual for Many Purposes'* in which Hekate is petitioned during the drowning of a cat. This spell interestingly, makes the cat's body a vessel for a god form and calls upon a cat-spirit by several god-names, including Hekate. Here we see a combination of these Anatolian connections: her appellation as a mother goddess, her feline associations, her identification with Dionysos, and her links to the dead:

> *'I call upon you, Mother of All Men, you who have held in your arms the limbs of Meliouchois (Dionysos/Mithras)* OROBASTRIA, NEBOUTOSOUALEETH, *Arkyia (Entrapper) Nekyia (Mistress of Corpses) Hermes, Hekate, Hermekate,* LEETH, AMOUMAMOUTERMYOR, *I conjure you, the daimon that has been aroused in this place.'*[58]

A further spell PGM VI (2622-2707) identifies Hekate with Selene, and instructs burning frankincense, bay, myrtle and cinnamon alongside more unsavoury ingredients such as dog embryos, goat fat, and the *'blood of a dead virgin'*. It is worth noting that such ingredients, when listed in spells, are not usually 'offerings' per se but magical items, to which either good or bad

---

[56] Vikki Bramshaw, Dionysos: Exciter to Frenzy
[57] Vikki Bramshaw, Dionysos: Exciter to Frenzy
[58] PGM III ('Magical Handbook') 1-164, The Greek Magical Papyri in Translation

were attracted. The same could be said of the cat of PGM III (1-164), in which the drowned cat is not an 'offering' to the gods but in fact, utilised as an *object* required for the spell. This is perhaps some insight into bull sacrifice and rites such as the *Taurobolium*, which whilst considered an offering to Kybele were also a means to an end - a magical operation to 'compel' a deity to act in our favour. This sort of sacrifice was portrayed in the TV series *Rome*, during which the niece of Julius Caesar sacrifices a bull in the Taurobolium to ensure the safety of her son. Offerings were not regarded in the same way that they are today; they involved both *'coercive offerings'* (to compel or even force a spirit or deity to act) and *'beneficent offerings'* (to honour a spirit or deity) such offerings are explained in PGM VI (2622-2707). Other sacrifices were made to coerce spirits or phantoms. A love spell, PGM IV (1390-1495) uses the offering of bread to call upon the souls of the dead *'those who have died untimely deaths and those dead violently'* with the aid of a terrifying manifestation of Hekate, *'Lady of the night Who feeds on filth, grim-eyed, dreadful...O Mistress Hekate.'*

However, spell sacrifices did not always involve the letting of blood or the conjuring of the dead. Spells such as the *Bear Charm* PGM IV (1275-1322) describe making simple burnt offerings such as incense and nuts together with figurative sacrifices (such as abstention from food, sex, meat, etc). This charm is considered to invoke Hekate, who was associated with the star constellation of the Bear; she is also addressed by name in another *Bear Charm* PGM VII (686-702) as *'Brimo, Earth Breaker'* which, we have already identified, was also an epithet of Kybele.

Hekate's role in magic is one of her more familiar virtues and perhaps linked to her Anatolian roots as a mediator to the unknown realms, liminal places, and the ecstatic. The term 'ecstatic' finds its roots in the Greek word *ekstasis* meaning *'to stand outside oneself'* referring to the sense of being absent from one's body; the feeling experienced during deity possession and theurgy. The dictionary meaning of the word ecstasy continues as *'a religious frenzy or trance-like state'*, and *'one involving a mystic self-transcendence'*. The practice of god-possession was almost entirely unique to the cults of Dionysos and Kybele[59] and not usually found in the worship of any of the Olympian Gods; people would worship them, but not seek to 'become' them. In comparison, the likes of the cult of Dionysos actively sought to merge man with god in a primal and ecstatic way, something that was alien to the people of Athens and considered barbaric – but would have been quite at home in places such as Egypt, Northern Europe or West Africa where god possession went hand-in-hand with effective magic. Dionysos was frequently referred to as the 'god of orgies' with the word *orgy* finding its origins in the Greek *orgia*, meaning *'ecstatic rites'* - energy-filled ritual methods including wild drumming and dancing, the use of intoxication, blood control and breath work (such as 'ritual hissing', found frequently in the PGM). These were all methods of raising energy and/or causing an 'absence' from the body, to allow a spirit to enter or facilitate communication with the otherworlds. This process was called *Enthousiasmos* meaning *'possessed by a god'* or, *'god-inspired'*, and was usually accompanied by oracular messages, wild deity-driven movements and chthonic forms of magic. These practices were described as 'uncivilised' by many Greek writers and referred to as 'low' magic, although arguably, would probably have been the outcome of many of the operations described in texts such as the PGM. Another practice common in both Dionysian and Hekatean magic was the use of spinning or swinging tools. One such method was *Aletis*, the practice of swinging back and forth on a swinging seat which led to visions and prophesies.[60] This practice was associated with raising the spirits of the dead or *shade*s (ghosts) and, as with other forms of ecstatic rites, assisted the spirits on a journey between one world and the other. *Iacchos*, one of the later guises of Dionysos, was referred to as the guiding

---

[59] Vikki Bramshaw, Dionysos: Exciter to Frenzy
[60] Vikki Bramshaw, Dionysos: Exciter to Frenzy

light and psychopomp for this sort of process and linked him to Hekate's torch-bearing role; their relationship in this respect would be made clear in the Rites of Eleusis. Another device, a magical wheel known as the *Rhombos*, was spun in a circular motion to aid a change of consciousness in a similar way[61] whilst the *Strophalos* was spun during the rites of Hekate and acted as a vehicle to communicate with otherworldly beings.

As liminal deities, Kybele, Hekate and Dionysos stood between the worlds and were not fixed to any one form or place; they signified freedom from limitation, they were animating powers who connected all living things. As such they were also effective shapeshifting gods; in fact Kybele was the only Phrygian goddess shown in anthropomorphic form[62] whilst Hekate was known for her multiple guises including the horse, the dog, and the snake. The Greek poet Nonnus wrote how Dionysos too, would also transform into a myriad of forms; *'a lion, a bull, a boar, a bear, a panther, a snake, and now a tree, fire, water.'*[63] With one foot in the world of the potential and another in the world of the physical, these deities traversed the states of spirit and matter.

Neither earthbound nor heavenbound, they lay somewhere in between. It is here, in the role of mediator, creatrix, and destroyer, that Hekate and Kybele find their common ground; overseeing all of life's transformative processes; the notion of 'becoming'. Whilst they almost certainly had their separate root origins, through a process of syncretism the two deities grew to become greater than the sum of their two parts. Kybele and Hekate would become mothers of state, overseers of armies, and protectors of city gates. They were mediators between the worlds and maintained control over heaven, earth, and sea. They were entangled in grass-roots magic surrounding primary concerns, such as obtaining meat and milk. They controlled and dominated

---

[61] Robert Brown, The Great Dionysiac Myth Vol. 1
[62] Birgitte Bøgh, The Phrygian Background of Kybele
[63] Nonnus, Dionysiaca c.500CE

the natural world, so important to our ancestors in the battle between the paradoxical states of the wild and the tame, of life and death, and all those liminal threshold places in-between.

At their most basic, they were even the landscape itself; the foreboding, fearful, fruitful, beautiful mountainsides of Anatolia, that reached up to the heavens where birds of prey circled, and leopards prowled. As we have shown, the mother goddess is a greater force of heaven and earth than perhaps we know to date.

Iberia at the Crossroads

Contributed by Ness Bosch, Scotland, UK

Iberia: the last frontier of the Mediterranean, a gateway between seas and cultures, a place of passage and cradle of gods and peoples. The Iberian Peninsula, the current Spain and Portugal territory, has been a crossroads for cultures throughout history. Surprisingly, the archaeological wealth of Iberia and its protohistory continues to be largely unknown. The peninsula had an important monumental megalithic culture; many of these monuments are much older than remains found, for example, in the British Isles or France. However, little is said about them outside academic circles and their historical importance is mostly ignored.

Local populations flourished in settlements spread throughout the peninsula, perhaps with the Castro Culture, as one of the most important exponents in the northwest. Iberia was an amalgamation of tribes and settlements, perhaps not very structured in comparison with the societies of the Levant and the Eastern Mediterranean. With the arrival of traders from the East in different waves, the peninsula underwent what is known as Orientalization. But this is not something that happened overnight, there is still debate about it and will be for years to come. Phoenicians did not arrive and settle, just like that. It is believed that trade contacts and expeditions in Iberia could have occurred hundreds of years before the establishment of formal colonies, and before the Phoenicians, the Mycenaeans also arrived in Iberia and established contacts with the locals. Iberia became a crossroads and the base between the Mediterranean, the Atlantic and the trade routes to the north. It is important to make the point that the arrival of the Phoenicians in Iberia marked an important revolution at a social, cultural, and commercial level. I grew up in an old Phoenician settlement on the coast of Granada, the old Seks-Sexi, modern Almuñecar, surrounded by Phoenician sites and it is something they taught us at school. Although I have to admit that they told us very little about the protohistoric religion, the gods of the Phoenicians, later the Romans, and the gods of Iberia in general before Christianization.

This introduction will help you to understand the importance and liminality of the Iberian Peninsula in the ancient Mediterranean. Perhaps it is also due to this liminal character of Iberia being between oceans and worlds, that the Goddess Hekate has become a popular deity among neopagans and polytheists in the Iberian Peninsula today, but this connection with Hekate is deeper than a mere geographical position.

At first glance, it may be difficult for us to establish a relationship between Hekate and Iberia. It is peculiar that although there seem to be no historical references to a possible Hekate cult in Iberia, one of the most important and possibly oldest local Goddesses of the peninsula, the Goddess Ataecina, (also known as Ataegina, Ategina, Adaecina, Adegina, as we find her name spelt in various ways under different epigraphs) shares many aspects of Hekate. Without people realising it, perhaps, Hekate's notoriety in modern Iberia could be because of the connection with Ataecina. Let's dig into this!

The bulk of the Ataecina cult extended approximately between the Betic System in Andalusia and the Central System, extending towards the West, entering what is now the territory of Portugal. Although we know that her cult spread to other parts of the peninsula, it is between the rivers Tajo, Guadiana, and Guadalquivir where most of the votive offerings, stelae, and dedications to the Goddess have been found, as well as defixions. We find her most important sanctuary in El Trampal, Cáceres but we know that at least one of her devotees travelled to the island of Sardinia, where he left her name in a dedication on the Mediterranean island.

Ataecina shares with Hekate the same chthonic character, she is also a Water Goddess, not only because of the connection to the waters in the underworld, underground, but also because Ataecina is a Goddess related to healing and magical arts. She is also linked to oracular work like Hekate and Ataecina is also seen as a Triple Goddess. She is a funerary Goddess but she is also a Life-giving deity, mainly because as a Chthonic Goddess, she is also responsible for everything that sleeps underground, including the seeds that will sow life on the surface. Her very own name means something like *'the one who has been born again'*.

> DEA ATAECINA
> TURI/BRIG(ENSIS) PROSERPINA
> PER TUAM MAIESTATEM
> TE ROGO ORO OBSECRO
> UTI VINDICES QUOT MIHI
> FURTI FACTUM EST QUISQUIS
> MIHI IMUDAVIT INVOLAVIT
> MINUSVE FECIT [E]A[S RES]
> Q(UAE) I(NFRA) S(CRIPTA) S(UNT)
> TUNICAS VI [--- P]AENULA
> LINTEA II IN[DUS]IUM CU/IUS
> [---]M IGNORO / [---]IUS

Defixio found in Emerita Augusta, modern Merida

She has a strong agricultural character and is also related to goats and livestock. Many of the votive offerings found dedicated to Ataecina were small bronzed-shaped goats, giving rise to debate whether the goat could be the original form of the Goddess or a way to substitute or simulate the sacrifice of a goat to the deity. She might even be a shapeshifting goddess, like Hekate herself. At this point, nothing in this relationship would shock me, as they are close.

Whilst some believe that Ataecina is possibly a local deity who evolved from a Bronze Age Goddess, others think that Ataecina is a composite Goddess who arose from different emanations of deities from the East. This is very possible actually.

If we look to the Mediterranean, not only do we find a connection between Ataecina with Hekate but with other Goddesses as well. It is no coincidence that the Romans in Iberia tried to syncretize Ataecina with Proserpina/Persephone. We find the name of Ataecina linked to Proserpina in several epigraphs. Of course, we can also find a subtle relationship between Ataecina and Demeter, the two sharing dominance over agriculture. It is astonishing how we find fused in one single deity, the Eleusinian Triad of Goddesses: Hekate, Persephone, and Demeter; that is something that I have always found fascinating about Ataecina.

In addition to the Persephone-Proserpina connection, we find in the Iberian Peninsula other goddesses that we can relate to Hekate in one way or another. For example, we find several inscriptions dedicated to Diana in Iberia, especially a very curious one where some angry dogs of the goddess are mentioned. It doesn't specifically say Hekate, but we do know that Hekate was part of the Diana Triformis triad along with Selene and Diana-Artemis. You may have come across references to a relationship between Diana and Hekate. The author Sorita d'Este has shared on several occasions details of her research and the connections between Hekate and Artemis of Ephesus, and I believe that the key to the origin of Hekate as we know her now could indeed be in Anatolia, even with some connection to Mesopotamia.

We cannot rule out that some of the references to Diana found in the Roman world refer to Hekate, as happens with other goddesses whose names are changed or named after one of their epithets. We even find objects where the goddess is referred to as Artemis-Hekate and among them some coins produced in Ecbatana, in ancient Iran.

Beyond this connection with Diana-Artemis, we find in Iberia another goddess with a triple character: the Matres. Some scholars have suggested there is a connection between the Matres and the triple form of God Lug-Lugus. And in the cult of Lug in Iberia, Lug is also closely linked to another bright God from the East: Apollo.

Now, let's keep digging a little deeper into the Iberian connections. At this point you should have a clear image of Iberia as a crossroads of cultures, and a knowledge that long before the Romans arrived, the Greeks and Phoenicians had, and founded different colonies throughout the peninsula. Before the Phoenicians settled in Iberia, they also founded colonies in Sardinia and Sicily. We know of the existence of temples to Astarte/Ishtar/Inanna in those Phoenician colonies and we know of the connection between Inanna and Persephone and the Goddesses of the underworld. And, of course, Sicily is the homeland of Persephone. It is very likely the Greeks could have also carried Hekate to their colonies. Perhaps it is not so wrong to think that Ataecina could be, as I say, a syncretism and evolution of a local deity with the deities that arrived in Iberia from the East. The similarities are evident. Even though we have little information about Ataecina in the Pre-Roman period, she managed to maintain her hegemony, even after the conquest and adhesion of the territory of Iberia - Hispania to the Roman Empire. We do not know if the future will gift us an archaeological find showing Ataecina related to Hekate.

Talking from personal experience I can say that Hekate has been a bridge deity for me, in the sense that she has brought me closer to other deities. I would have never imagined when I began to celebrate Hekate at her first 'Rite of Her Sacred Fires' that the Goddess would take me to so many places and open so many doors for me. But of course, at that time in 2010, I was just getting to know her and I didn't know that she is a 'Key'. Funnily enough, it was Hekate who guided me to Goddess Ataecina and I hadn't realised how much she had also been guiding my path to other gods until now. For years I dedicated myself exclusively to Hekate as her Priestess, also as a member of the Covenant of Hekate, as a Torchbearer, and as the head of a temple sanctuary in southern Spain. I was, let's say, all hers, until goddess Hekate herself began to lead me to other deities and gave me her blessing to open my temple space to other deities as well. That changed the course of my life. I remember the sensation perfectly. I noticed her taking a few steps back towards the shadows and as she moved aside, my work with the gods and goddesses changed forever. Of course, she did not leave, she has been popping in and out, from the shadows to the light. She just made space for other deities to approach me, which was decisive for my work, and to this day,Just Hekate is always omnipresent, among everything else.

Ataecina was one of the goddesses that came from her hand and after researching Hekate and other deities for years, exploring the sources available about Ataecina, it all made sense. I hope this text brings some interesting insights for you too.

Bibliography:

Agudo Villanueva, M. 2020 Hekate la Diosa Sombria. Editorial Dilema
d'Este Sorita. 2017. Circle for Hekate. Avalonia Books
Lopez Ruiz, Carolina. 2021 Phoenicians & the making of the Mediterranean.
    Harvard University Press
Rojas Gutiérrez M. Rocio. 2016, Ataecina, un análisis de la continuidad de los
    cultos locales o indígenas en la Hispania romana. LIGUSTINUS
    (Universidad de Sevilla).

Sacred Shakespeare:
The creation of Hekate Genesis

Contributed by Emily Carding, East Sussex, UK

> *In an experimental fusion of classical theatre and ritual, we will weave a tale of creation, conflict, destruction and rebirth using text from a number of Shakespeare's plays, including The Tempest, A Midsummer Night's Dream, Macbeth and Hamlet. In the beginning, the Universe is created with the words of power...these words bring the elements into being and through Hekate they face their darkness and chaos before being brought together into balance and harmony, revived by her sacred fires. This will be the first production by Emily Carding's Hermetic theatre company, 'SO POTENT ARTS', who work on the principle that all theatre has the potential to be an act of magic, and that all actors are magicians.*

Thus reads the promotional blurb for *Hekate: Genesis*, a half-hour piece of ritual theatre that I was commissioned to write and perform as part of the *Hekate Symposium* in May 2013. Since the timing coincided with the hectic depths of Term Three, with everyone (myself included) committed to several pieces, the circumstances for rehearsal were far less than ideal. The following chapter is a reflection on the creation of the mash-up ritual text, the compact yet experimental rehearsal process and the performance itself.

> *The overriding aesthetic question today is: what permutations and what contemporary insights can be fashioned from the body of work bequeathed us over 400 years of Shakespearean history? ...it might involve radical reorganisation of his actual materials- scenes, speeches, characters which are unmistakably Shakespearean but which, taken into other hands, are now transformed and put to other uses. (Marowitz 1991:30)*

The post-modern aesthetic of plundering Shakespeare and creating a mash-up text, as referred to by Charles Marowitz in the above quote (from a chapter provocatively titled *How to Rape Shakespeare*), is usually rendered with an irreverent, humorous, or sacrilegious intention. With *Hekate:Genesis* it was my intention to use this technique to create something sacred. In order to achieve this, an established ritual structure had to be in place as the foundation. Inspired by a spiritual pilgrimage to Sicily with Peter Dawkins and Mark Rylance in 2013 that I was privileged to participate in, which explored the mythopoetic and esoteric content of *The Winter's Tale*, I was able to use this play's innate magical structure of life, death and rebirth as a starting point. Then, drawing on the teachings of the *Chaldean Oracles*, the Bible and the Qabalah, slowly started to create a ritual piece from Shakespeare's words.

The *Chaldean Oracles* consists of Hellenistic commentary on fragments of a mystery poem. The worldview portrayed within these writings has much in common with Neo-platonism and Gnosticism, but interestingly Hekate takes on the mantle of the animating Cosmic Soul and 'Soteira' or 'saviour' who *ensouls the light, the fire, the aether and the Cosmoi* (Johnston 1990:62). This *celestial and beneficient* (Johnston 1990:143) goddess is in contrast to her portrayal in Macbeth as the primarily malevolent Queen of the Witches, Hekate's Chthonic form found in folklore and popular mythology. This aspect has been sadly neglected so far by others studying the magical side of Shakespeare's work, who see her only as a dark influence. Jill Line writes about Hekate's dark influence at length, saying that *when man chooses to ignore natural law and create war, disorder and havoc in himself...the binding force of love is forgotten and the chaos of Hekate takes over.* (Line 2004: 31) Though this may reflect the surface level of Shakespeare's interpretation of this ancient goddess, if we broaden our viewpoint to consider Hekate as the World Soul, then we can see her as Nature herself, who features as a dominant power throughout Shakespeare's plays. I argue that rather than influencing the events of the play overtly for the negative, Hekate appears at the moment of choice, illuminating the figurative crossroads. The darkness that makes the choice based on ego and ambition, or chaos and destruction comes from within the soul of the anti-hero, which leads to the redemption of the Land through their eventual destruction. In the end, the greater good of Nature is served, and Truth is revealed. Hekate is a multi-faceted Goddess, and since the event was dedicated to her function as Soteira and World Soul, this would be my focus for the piece.

I made a conscious decision to keep the cast as small as possible. I knew I needed at least three actors, to portray the triple-formed nature of Hekate, which *emphasised her power over the three realms, these being the heavens, sea and earth* (d'Este 2009: 19), but also that I would need the fourth element of Fire, which also encapsulates the power of Light and represents Soul. Since the four elements in this context related to aspects of the goddess Hekate, I knew these four needed to be female. Since the power of creation is made possible through the energy of polarity I chose to have a fifth actor who was not only male, but my then-husband - not a trained actor, but a trained magician. This was part of the experimental nature of my process, as I was curious to see whether it would be more effective in the context of ritual theatre to train actors in magical technique or magicians in theatrical technique. This lesson was learned quite quickly as I discovered in him a reluctance to learn lines, rehearse, or warm-up the voice before the performance. Though this could be put down to a stubborn personality, in fact it highlights the fact that actors, though the practice of transforming themselves through their work, are already part-way to becoming magicians, and tend to be more open to new techniques. Therefore, my focus will be on training actors in magical techniques rather than the contra.

GENESIS OF THE TEXT

Before piecing together the text it was necessary to compile an amount of raw material. This I did by searching Shakespeare's works for certain key words which related to the core ritual structure of creation, death and rebirth, the concept of polarity (male and female, light and dark, order and chaos) and the four elements. The first stage of the ritual structure would be the first sparks of creation itself, the descent of animating soul, or Hekate's sacred fire, into matter. This involves the division of the unknowable spiritual Source into two, akin to the descent of Sophia, Wisdom, the Shekinah or Holy Spirit, the feminine aspect of God. Using the entirety of Shakespeare's works as a source, it was helpful to use the post-modern resource of the internet to be able to search the texts for keywords which would lead to a selection of phrases and speeches which could be used, arranged or discarded as necessary. Some came easily without searching. For example, 'in the beginning' was always going to be 'words, words, words…', drawing inspiration from the creation myth of the bible and also representing the three stages of spirit's descent into matter - the Source united and whole, the split into polarity, and the animation of matter with sacred fire, creating the four elements. This also echoes the celestial hierarchy and concept of 'logos' in neo-platonic philosophy. These three stages were marked in the opening with the three actresses portraying Earth, Sea and Sky standing in a triple formation, each holding a Tibetan singing bowl and sounding a chime for each repetition. The first 'words' were spoken by the actor playing Source, alone. The second was spoken by Source and Light (Fire) together, to represent the initial split of one into two. The third was spoken by the whole cast, representing the division of spirit into the four elements and hence the world's creation.

With this small example of the deconstruction and re-application of text, it is possible to see how a change of context can add new significance to the structure of Shakespeare's language. 'Words, words, words...' is an iconic quote from Hamlet, and thus already carries some weight within popular culture and is likely to resonate on some level with any audience member who has a little knowledge of Shakespeare. Its triple structure lends a natural resonance to its new purpose, and as I scoured Shakespeare's works for more synchronous phrases and sections, I discovered not only phrases that could be used in almost direct opposition to their original context with great effect, but also a large amount of material which required little alteration to be used within a sacred context. Searching simply for words about words in Shakespeare led to so much raw material that there was no room in the scope of this text to use the majority of it, but the nature of the extracts illustrated clearly that the author was acutely aware of the potent effect that words could have in and on the world. The most surprisingly rich vein of spiritually significant word ore to be mined was to be found in Shakespeare's sonnets.

Sonnets 29 and 39 provided the majority of the symbolic dialogue between Source and Light during the initial split of one into two. Placing these words into a new context makes the underlying esoteric symbolism more apparent, and rather than reading them as love poetry, they start to take on a deeper meaning for the reader, whether or not the hidden depths were intentional. In *Shakespeare and the Goddess of Complete Being*, Ted Hughes theorises that the Dark Lady of the sonnets is in fact the Dark Goddess or Hekate in her aspect of Queen of Hell. This is clearly a creative interpretation, which may have no academic justification but is valid within a mythopoetic context. Inspired by this concept, I used Sonnet 130 set to original music as the mystical song that awakens the statue of Light in the final ritual stage of resurrection.

Returning to Shakespeare's plays as a source, there were three from which substantial sections formed the backbone of the piece, with smaller chunks of other plays fleshing out the body, and most plays at least contributing a line or two. These spinal plays were *The Tempest, A Midsummer Night's Dream* and *The Winter's Tale*, all of which obviously have an original magical context but brought very different elements to the mix.

The Tempest provided not only the very ending of the piece, with the 'Our revels now are ended' speech, but also a surprising Hekate connection. Prospero's invocation to the spirits of the land in Act V scene one, which begins *'Ye Elves of hills, brooks, standing lakes and groves'* is almost certainly directly inspired by Medea's invocation to Hekate from Ovid's *Metamorphoses*. Not only do we know that Ovid was one of Shakespeare's most frequently used sources for stories, but this speech follows the same structure of calling on spirits of the landscape, boasting of effects they can cause on the elements, the uprooting of trees and even the raising of the dead. Both speeches are written in a way that would be considered as effective invocation technique by a trained magician.

The conflict between Titania and Oberon from *A Midsummer Night's Dream* provided the central section of the piece, in which the nature of polarity is explored. Since both Titania and Hekate are strongly linked to Diana, the moon goddess, and also considering that one of Hekate's aspects within British folklore is as a Fairy Queen, this had a strong resonance with the ritual purpose of the piece. Also used from this play were some of Puck's lines which list the forms that he takes, which also happen to be animal forms connected with Hekate: *'Sometime a horse I'll be, sometime a hound, A hog, a headless bear, sometime a fire...'*[64]

The Winter's Tale, which in itself abides by the ritual structure, provided the 'rebirth' segment of the piece with its final scene in which the statue of Hermione, long presumed dead, is brought to life. Other plays that contributed significant sections of text included *Othello, Hamlet,* and *Titus Andronicus*, which I was

---

[64] AMND, Act III, scene i

surprised to find, contained some very useful elemental material. Here is an example of how a speech, (Titus Andronicus Act III scene one), was broken down into its elemental components and lines assigned accordingly:

> *Darkness: If there were reason for these miseries,*
> *Then into limits could I binde my woes:*
> *Sea: When heaven doth weep,*
> *Earth: ..doth not the earth o'erflow?*
> *Sky: If the winds rage,*
> *Sea: doth not the sea wax mad?*
> *I am the sea;*
> *Sky: hark, how her sighs do blow!*
> *Earth: She is the weeping welkin, I the earth:*
> *Sea: Then must my sea be moved with her sighs;*
> *Earth: Then must my earth with her continual tears*
> *Sea: Become a deluge, overflow'd and drown'd;*
> *Earth: For why my bowels cannot hide her woes,*
> *Sea: But like a drunkard must I vomit them.*
> *Sky: Then give me leave, for losers will have leave*
> *To ease their stomachs with their bitter tongues.*

The cycling through the elements, which is inherent in the text in its intact state, lends itself naturally to a rhythm suited to ritual and this proved to work well in a number of cases.

INNOVATING REHEARSAL METHODS

The ideal circumstances for rehearsing a piece of this nature would include a month, (or one full cycle of the moon) of the cast living and working together, in various landscapes and with the meditations and exercises suggested in the third chapter. However, due to various mitigating circumstances, we had five days, during which time members of the cast, myself included, also had other commitments. These constraints resulted in the need to distil the experiment and filter ideas down to those that seemed most essential and which it was hoped would work towards the desired effect in as short a space of time as possible. The cast was a mix of abilities. Sea and Sky were played by two fellow theatre students with no previous experience of magical work, Earth was played by a very experienced actress who has worked mostly in the chorus of West End musicals and also had a good deal of magical experience, and I took the role of Light/Fire. Source/Darkness was played by my then-husband who is magically trained but is not an actor, and due to work commitments barely participated in the rehearsal process. This meant that the women formed a strong connection through working together and he remained apart, which although it weakened his performance, created an interesting energetic dynamic of polarity, which worked for the piece.

The rehearsal process can be broken down into the following core elements:

COMMUNAL LIVING

The cast all lived under the same roof for the rehearsal process to encourage a strong energetic connection and to enable flexible rehearsal hours. Cast member Sarah Green, who played Sea, reflected back on the process and remarked that *"...living in close quarters during the process really helped form a quick but healthy bond between performers."*

MEDITATION

Guided visualisations were performed with the cast in order to familiarise them with the qualities of the element they would be representing in the piece in order that they might be more readily able to channel that energy in performance. This was particularly aimed at the two most magically inexperienced members of the cast, who were open-minded yet nervous about something so out of the ordinary, as noted by Sarah Green, who recalls:

"I was very unsure on the meditations as I always found myself quite cynical and I was nervous about something I

> *didn't know much about. Once I settled into it though it was interesting to see where I rested with my own element and how I subconsciously view water and what water situations I prefer deep down. It was also interesting to note similarities I had with Dana, someone I am close friends with, and what pictures our minds conjured."*

The meditations were complemented by Glynn Macdonald's elemental postures from our Globe training, which we also incorporated into one of the more overtly ritualised sections of the performance, as the elements are called in to bless the space.

SACRED SPACE

Each session would begin with a group ritual calling in the seven directions to bless the space and end with thanking them in order to maintain a sacred space through the process and to aid in focus for the short, intensive rehearsal period.

OUTDOOR LOCATIONS

> *"Given our roles as elements being close to nature really helped me to engage and explore 'water' and its relationship with the other elements. Rehearsing on the beach was especially fun and engaging as it really felt like you were speaking these lines in the elements themselves."- Sarah Green*

If solely using meditation or visualisation to connect with elemental energies there is a danger of the experience becoming too intellectualised and 'stuck in the head'. In order to strengthen the connection with the elements and ground the experience in a more immediate way, rehearsals and movement devising sessions were held in outdoor locations pertinent to each element. These included the beach, moorland and local standing stones.

MASK WORK

Masks were utilised in order to free the actors from their usual personas and to aid transformational work and add a ritualised feel. The masks were not neutral, but rather particular to each elemental realm of Earth, Sea and Sky. Cast member Sarah Green noted that the use of masks freed her as a performer, saying that *"As someone who can be quite shy in life and as a performer I found it very liberating to wear the mask and take on the character."* Since in this case the masks were pre-existing, it would be an intriguing further step in future experiments to take the time for actors to create their own masks as a group within a ritual space.

COLOUR SYMBOLISM AND SPECTACLE

In addition to the masks, each element had a coloured dancing veil which they kept with them at all times during the rehearsal process. These represented the different elemental colours- yellow for air/Sky, blue for water/Sea, and green for Earth - and since they were incorporated into the devised movement created a visual spectacle. With the thought of the transportative power of spectacle in mind, we adapted a pair of red Isis wings, a type of veil used in belly dance, by sewing fairy lights into the hem. This created stunning visual effects when used in darkness, which we exploited during the closing resurrection sequence during an improvised dance, which we encouraged the audience to join.

DEVISING

Though the creation of the text and rituals was a solo effort, the movement within the piece was group-led and devised. This added a greater sense of ownership of the piece within the cast, and also required a greater depth of familiarity with the meaning of the words in order that the right feeling and energies were conveyed than would be necessary within a more dictated director-led process.

THE PERFORMANCE

Due to the nature of the event there was no time to rehearse in the actual performance space. The rehearsals in different locations had prepared the cast for this, and Sarah Green insightfully noted that *"Rather than be a hindrance it made it really feel like this ephemeral one-time piece that was offered to the gathering and was gone."*

References:

The full video of Hekate:Genesis can be viewed here:
https://www.youtube.com/watch?v=lxIejl95CZs

Further reading: Ovid's Metamorphoses: Book VII 179-233

Medea's invocation to Hekate- similarities to Propero's *'Ye Elves'* highlighted in italics

> *Night, most faithful keeper of our secret rites;*
> Stars, that, with the golden moon, succeed the fires of light;
> Triple Hecate, you who know all our undertakings,
> *and come, to aid the witches' art, and all our incantations:*
> You, Earth, who yield the sorceress herbs of magic force:
> You, airs and breezes, pools and hills, and every watercourse;
> Be here; all you Gods of Night, and Gods of Groves endorse.
> *Streams, at will, by banks amazed, turn backwards to their source.*
> I calm rough seas, and stir the calm by my magic spells:
> bring clouds, disperse the clouds, raise storms and storms dispel;
> and, with my incantations, I break the serpent's teeth;
> *and root up nature's oaks, and rocks, from their native heath;*
> *and move the forests, and command the mountain tops to shake,*
> *earth to groan, and from their tombs the sleeping dead to wake.*
> You also, Luna, I draw down, eclipsed, from heaven's stain,
> though bronzes of Temese clash, to take away your pains;
> and at my chant, the chariot of the Sun-god, my grandsire,

grows pale: Aurora, at my poisons, dims her morning fire.
You quench the bulls' hot flame for me: force their necks to bow,
beneath the heavy yoke, that never pulled the curving plough:
You turn the savage warfare, born of the serpent's teeth,
against itself, and lull the watcher, innocent of sleep;
that guard deceived, bring golden spoil, to the towns of Greece.
Now I need the juice by which old age may be renewed,
that can regain the prime of years, return the flower of youth,
and You will grant it. Not in vain, stars glittered in reply:
not in vain, winged dragons bring my chariot, through the sky.'

Entering the Temple of Medea:
Hero Cult, Spiritual Ancestry & Hekatean Devotion

Contributed by B.P. Shoop, Northern Virginia, USA

Medea Shrine, B.P. Shoop

Medea, the Colchian Sorceress, has fascinated secular, religious and scholarly audiences alike for thousands of years. With her daring feats, strength, and mastery of mystical arts, she has inspired the world of art and literature and become a cultural icon for many, but she represents something quite unique to Hekatean communities and devotees. Medea's worship and devotion to the Goddess Hekate has served as source material, history, and inspiration for so many of us looking to connect our own worship of Hekate to tradition and the ancient world. And yet, while Medea has solidified her position as a cultural icon, she has not been given her rightful place in the modern pantheon of pagan revivals. Though some of us have incorporated her into our practices, many still view her solely as an archetypal or narrative figure. In light of this, I wish to use this piece to encourage Hekate devotees to explore veneration of our predecessor in devotion and incorporate Medea into their practices. I propose that by shifting our view of Medea from one of a literary character to that of a hero, her place beside Hekate in a modern cult becomes much clearer.

HERO CULT

For anyone looking into the practice of, or practices influenced by, Ancient Greek religious traditions the hero cult is an essential concept to understanding this region's ancient religious landscape. Unfortunately, interest and resurrection of hero cults have not been very central, often not included at all, in modern attempts at the revival of ancient polytheistic religions. From an ancient perspective, this leaves quite a gap in any reconstruction of Ancient Greek traditions.

In the Ancient Greek conception, heroes were *'real or putative human beings who had lived human lives, had performed some extraordinarily great or awful deeds…then unlike the common dead, received public cult at their tombs'*[65].

These public cults of the heroic dead would have been extremely common and incredibly important for the average Ancient Greek. While most modern pagan attempts at the revival and reconstruction of Ancient Greek religious traditions - apart from hardline reconstructionists - focus almost exclusively on the veneration of the gods of the ancient world, for most ancient Greeks the worship of heroes were often much more central to their daily, regular worship than the larger gods of myth - at least more central than we tend to see today in neo-pagan

---

[65] Mikalson, 2010, p. 38

communities. There are likely many reasons for this, but one clear one is that, to the Ancient Greeks,

> "...gods are remote, the heroes are near at hand" (Burkert, 1985, p. 207). However, I do not wish to indicate that the worship of heroes and gods was oppositional or separate by any means. Heroes, as we can see in the myths of figures like Herakles and Asklepios, were often connected to the gods in their cults and stories, often descending more or less directly from the divine. They may have even been priests or devotees of certain gods. For example, a "hero...might receive a place in a god's sanctuary because he originated the festival or worship of that deity, as Erechtheus had the Panathenaea at Athens for Athena Polias" (Mikalson, 2010, p. 44).

Heroes, like the gods, were given offerings at their holy sites and prayed to for a number of different purposes. Often, hero cults served both religious and cultural/community functions, both being prayed to for material improvements to the life of the worshipper while simultaneously serving as an ancestral figure who might connect groups of people in their local communities or city-states (Mikalson, 2010, p. 41). In exchange for blessings in their life - or to appease angry heroes - typical chthonic offerings of wine, milk, blood, and honey would have been offered to them at their tombs, called *heroa* (Mikalson, 2010, p. 38). Heroes were often worshipped for the same reasons as the gods: in the hope that the divine figure might bring the worshipper good health, good fortune, protection, or any other blessing a god might give (Mikalson, 2010, p. 41). Heroes and their cults were thus essential components of everyday life for the Ancient Greeks, and could benefit us immensely as those who aim to reconstruct or revive ancient Greek religious traditions.

MEDEA AS HERO

But if Medea is not typically considered to be amongst the heroic pantheon of the ancient world, how can we conceive of her as one today? Medea fits much, if not all, of the criteria of what qualifies a figure as a 'hero'. Firstly, she is descended from the divine, being the granddaughter of Helios. Secondly, she also performed many great, and sometimes awful, deeds in aiding Jason's quest for the Golden Fleece, so much so that according to a few sources she has her afterlife in Elysium and is married to Achilles (Apollonius of Rhodes, 1971, p. 169). Her power was fabled for thousands of years, purportedly being able to *'put out a raging fire...stop rivers as they roar in spate, arrest a star, and check the movement of the sacred moon'* (Apollonius of Rhodes, 1971, p. 123). Furthermore, she may have received worship in antiquity. While many are familiar with the story of the revenge taken by Medea as told by Euripides, there were other, and earlier, versions of her tale:

According to one, Medeia took each of her children in turn to the sanctuary of Hera to 'hide them away' (*katakruptein*) thinking that this operation would make them immortal. (The word may mean she buried them). When Jason discovered what she had done, he abandoned her. Another version held that Medeia instructed her children to bring a poisoned robe to her rival Glauke. *'When Glauke perished...the enraged Korinthians stoned the innocent children'.* (Larson, 2007, p. 34).

After this came to pass, supposedly the children started causing Corinthian infants to die, and so they began to make sacrifices to the children. The sacrifices, however, *'may have been conducted for Medeia herself, since some scholars view her as a divine figure whose cult was superseded by Hera's'* (Larson, 2007, p. 35). While this ancient cult connected to the health and wellbeing of children might be very different from the cult of Medea we might wish to construct today as Hekate devotees, it still provides us a basis for understanding Medea in the heroic and religious role.

In constructing a modern hero cult, we might turn to Medea for numerous functions. Medea could be prayed to as a divine figure who delivers justice, understanding her wrath as one which is just against those who wronged her or others and broke oaths made before the gods. She also, according to Diodorus (cited in Ogden, 2009, p. 79) freed men from unjust sentences given out by her father. We might also understand her as a saviour, like Hekate, for her repeated saving of those in need. Diodorus tells us '[t]*hey report that Medea learned all the powers of drugs from [Hekate] and [Kirke], but her own inclination was the opposite. For she continually saved strangers put in danger.*' Furthermore, she continuously saves Jason from the many perils on his quests. She may also be looked to as an avenging spirit, one who exacts punishment upon those who wronged her devotees, or a champion of women and those who face marginalisation (particularly immigrants, as she herself was one).

Finally, she might serve as a hero of witches and occultists. We might view her as a spirit which could assist us in the mystical arts, granting us guidance and power in our practices. In this way she resembles the goddess she serves, whose name was often used in the incantations and prayers of Medea. Similar to figures like Aradia who was said to bring magic from her divine ancestry to humanity, Medea becomes a saviour or hero to those magically inclined. However, these roles are not exhaustive, and further examination of her mythos might glean even more potential cultic functions for the modern devotee.

MEDEA VENERATION AND HEKATEAN DEVOTION

Hero worship and veneration were also historically important components of the worship of gods, and often found in connection to the worship of a god. As mentioned previously, heroes might be associated with a god for a number of reasons, being a founder of a god's cult or festival, descent from that god, a romantic relationship with that god, or may have even been killed by that god (Mikalson, 2010, p. 44). Synthesising scholarly and spiritual approaches to analysing the functions of a hero cult, we might understand the worship of heroes in connection to the divine serving as a means to further connect the worshipper with the gods and divine forces.

As mentioned above, the heroes seemed to be closer to the average ancient Greek than the gods tended to be. While this might relate to a potential difference between civic and personal religion, we could also interpret this understanding as a kind of metaphysical hierarchy. As heroes were typically understood as spirits of the dead, as opposed to gods themselves (with the exception of figures like Herakles and Asklepios), we might be able to view them as in closer proximity to a devotee than deity typically is - whereas gods, on the other hand, might be more distant from us at times. Perhaps we could interpret this closeness to the heroic dead as a key reason for their significance in spirituality. Heroes could be seen to serve as intermediaries between us and the gods, and so by honouring them and building relationships with them, we gain more direct access to the realm of the divine through our connections with heroes. While this is just a theory, and there are complications when it comes to the opposition between the dead and the ouranic gods, in the case of Hekate it seems to be quite a reasonable conclusion.

Hekate, whose nature was at times chthonic and was believed to reside in the Underworld, or at least able to travel there, was often invoked in binding tablets. Binding tablets, which sought the aid of chthonic powers, were often disposed of in graves with the dead (Ogden, 2009, p. 210). By burying these tablets with the deceased, *'the soul of the deceased was expected to hand over, like a letter, to [the chthonic god] the messages scratched on these tablets'* (Mikalson, 1983, p. 77). This logic about the dead serving as intermediaries between gods and humans could be applied rather easily to making sense of the relationship between a hero and divine chthonic powers. If we are to apply this principle to the relationship between Medea and Hekate, it becomes clear why one might seek to develop a devotional practice to Medea. By honouring her, forming a relationship with her, and getting into her good graces, she might serve as a beneficent intermediary between a devotee and the goddess Hekate. Medea veneration could, then, be thought of as strengthening our relationships with Hekate, inferring that Medea might intercede on our behalf, or, like many other intermediaries such as daemones, bring our prayers and offerings to Hekate, and bring Her messages and aid to us. Understanding Medea veneration as a bridge between us and the goddess to whom we are devoted reveals the benefit we might receive as Hekate devotees by giving devotion to Her ancient priestess as well.

From a practical and intellectual perspective as well, developing a modern hero worship of Medea provides us with opportunities to revisit primary sources, scholarship, and tradition to expand and shape our practices. Many of us are introduced to polytheistic spirituality through popular sources representative of a new pagan viewpoint, but Medea challenges us to look beyond this. As mentioned above, hero cult and Medea veneration are rarely, if ever, the topic of modern instructional pagan literature, and in an era ever increasingly concerned with innovation and eclecticism, being relegated to historical and primary sources to begin to craft this practice may actually be a blessing in disguise. It requires us to return to square one and begin again with the basics of devotion. We have to revisit the epics and mythological narratives in their primary form to gain often niche but significant information about the figure of our devotion. What were their symbols, their heroic deeds, their lineages, etc? Likewise, we must consult scholarship on ancient Greek religion to begin to understand how to actually craft a devotional practice to a heroic figure. What offerings were given? How were they given? Under what circumstances were these figures approached? By having to rely on this material, we put ourselves back through the challenges of research in the name of devotion, which is sure to bring us many rewards. This might provide us with an ever-needed balance in our spiritual journeys, that we might root ourselves in history and tradition in order to move forward.

In the case of seeking to strengthen our devotion to Hekate through the veneration of Medea, these rewards would be doubled. Medea's literary appearances are filled with rich depictions of ancient Hekatean devotion. By revisiting or being introduced to these pieces, we (re)familiarize ourselves with ancient tradition, learning how devotees, like Medea, worshipped Hekate in antiquity. We learn from these epics the protocols for ritual purity and cleansing, invocation, offering, and prayer in the ancient world, allowing us to reconnect ourselves and our practices to tradition. This research, in turn, is sure to revitalise, strengthen, and grow our relationships with the goddess Hekate, regardless of where in that journey we are. What may be the most transformative shift in Hekatean devotion through the incorporation of Medea veneration, though, is the identification with a spiritual ancestry or lineage. Heroes, as discussed above, often functioned as the figure of a common ancestor whose worship delineated, and sometimes constituted, membership to specific groups, families, communities, and city-states. Medea would be no different. A scholiast on Aristophanes' *Clouds* expressed that *'The Thessalians are slandered as sorcerers... And even still in our own day the women of Thessaly are called witches (pharmakides). And they say that, when fleeing, Medea cast out...a chest of drugs (pharmaka) there and they flourished'* (cited in Ogden, 2009, p. 315). Daniel Ogden describes this passage as *'making Medea and her drugs the direct originator of Thessalian witchcraft'* (2009, p. 315). Extrapolating from this passage, we can understand Medea as the origin of a magical and devotional practice focused on service to the goddess Hekate, one which we, as modern Hekate devotees, are descendants of. In this way, we follow in the footsteps of figures such as Simaetha who invokes the name of Hekate, but also of Medea, who served as an archetype for her magical practice, carrying on a tradition of devotion and magic from antiquity to today.

While so many of us experience our practices on our own, often isolated from other practitioners, in a world ravaged by divisions and conflict, seeking commonality through understanding ourselves as inheritors of Medea's tradition allows us to form community through hero cult just as the ancients did.

We can draw on this lineage and history in our practices, naming ourselves as descendants of Medea and her tradition, not by blood, but by devotion and spirit. Framing devotion to Hekate through the experiences of devotion to Medea, and vice versa, unites us in a new way and crafts a new viewpoint on Hekeatean tradition simultaneously rooted in antiquity and modernity. This reframing teaches us the importance of innovation in combination with tradition in devotional and magical practice, and helps us to view the divine, the ancients, and each other in a more collective way. Rather than seeing ourselves as different people with different practices surrounding the same goddess, Medea veneration helps us to see each other as spiritual relatives, carrying on different offshoots of an ancient tradition.

Hekate &
the Brazilian Crossroads

Contributed by Francine Derschner, Brazil

Rite of Her Sacred Fires in São Paulo, Brazil, 2019

When it was suggested I write about Hekate's cult in South America, especially in Brazil my native country, my first reaction was shock. I was really intrigued by the fact that other devotees might have an interest in reading about the devotional practices of a peripheral country with no traditional association with this Goddess. To think about this theme was a journey that led me to review my own culture and to perceive from another angle our particularities in all their nuances. I do not intend to make a historical analysis of the emergence of the Goddess cult in the region, because, although there may be sources for the subject, they are unknown to me.

I think it is important to start by highlighting some general data about South America and my country to facilitate understanding of our current religious landscape. Geographic data tells us that South America has 17,819,100 km² of land, covering 12% of the land surface and 6% of the world's population. In this region, there are approximately twelve countries and seven territories. Our ethnic background consists predominantly of three ethnicities: Indians, whites, and blacks. The native indigenous population has been decimated for many centuries, and currently, only Peru and Bolivia have an indigenous ethnic majority.

Brazil has a significant African influence. Recent research estimates that nearly 5,800,000 Africans were brought here as slaves between 1501 and 1875[66]. Between 1889 and 1930[67] it also received a significant wave of European immigrants, mainly Italian, Spanish and Portuguese, totalling more than four million people. With this diversified ethnographic basis, it is not difficult to understand our equally diverse religious landscape. We are the largest Catholic nation in the world, with 64% of the population declaring themselves to be Roman Catholic[68]. A large part of the population is Christian evangelicals, and many are practitioners of religions of African origin, especially Candomblé and Umbanda. The government does not yet officially account for the Spiritist and Pagan communities.

In Brazil these different religions converge, creating new cults just as our different ethnicities also gave birth to a unique mixed population. Candomblé and Umbanda are Brazilian religions - Candomblé cults exist in Africa but not with the denominations and configuration of the Brazilian Candomblé. When the enslaved people arrived in Brazil, they went through a process of forced catechization, which included not only the acceptance of Catholicism as a religion but also the widespread adoption of European Christian names through baptism.

It was within this context, with the prohibition of the realisation of their native religious cults, that enslaved Africans

---

[66] Data provided by the slavevoyages database
[67] See André Luiz Lanza and Maria Lucia Lamounier
[68] Data provided by the IBGE regarding the Demographic Census of 2010

were forced to adapt their practices and mix them with Catholicism, associating Orixás with Catholic saints like Ogum and Saint George, Jesus Christ and Oxalá or Iansã and Santa Barbara - a purposive religious syncretism that aimed at the preservation of the African religiosity and created the Candomblé.

Umbanda provides our best example of a typically Brazilian religion. It emerged in the early 20th century in southeastern Brazil, and is based on the synthesis of distinct religious movements such as Candomblé, Catholicism and Spiritism.

For a long time, an attempt was made in the country to unite Umbanda and Spiritism, to create one movement, since it has as its primary practices the connection with the spirits and charity - principles central to Spiritist doctrine. However, this attempt at artificial unification concealed a racist undertone, which aimed to keep Umbanda out of its African origins. Fortunately, the attempt failed, but Umbanda ended up dividing from there, and today we speak about different lines of Umbanda. On the one hand, there is the so-called 'pure umbanda', 'umbanda limp', 'umbanda branca' or 'umbanda de white line' in the sense of 'white magic', and on the other, the cult of the so-called 'black line', also with the meaning of 'black magic'. It is worth mentioning that, as a reflection of this division, almost every influence of the African rites was relegated to the black line, which was seen by its opponents as an evil-linked and less evolved side.

But not only the African-born religions created their own versions in Brazil. Catholicism underwent a transformation in our national territory and began to be characterized by a greater permeability to external practices. Of course, this process was not welcomed by the Catholic Church of the early settlers, but with time and popular appeal, the Church did not have much choice. To talk a little more about this phenomenon and the relationship of the Brazilians with the magic that allowed the arrival and acceptance of the Hekate cult today, we need to discuss the 'arrival' of witchcraft in the country.

For this, we will return to the beginning of the Brazilian colonial period. At that time, religiosity in the country was centred in the hands of the great landlords and their families. Due to the distance of the colony from Europe, the Church showed little interest in Brazilian souls, with only one official diocese in the country. The mission to catechise the native and African peoples was thus granted to the settlers and some Jesuits. Initially, Indigenous religiosity remained restricted to the forests and African cults to the slave quarters, but it was precisely this distance from the main headquarters of the Church that contributed to a greater loosening of Catholic dogmas in the country. To control slave labour, whether black or indigenous, many of the slave-holders used a syncretic religiosity with which their captives could identify, thus avoiding revolts that could arise with the total eradication of their original cults. In this context, the cult of Saint Benedict, a dark-skinned Moorish saint who was only to be officialised by the Catholic Church in 1743, was already practised in Brazil as the holy protector of the slaves. We also have the appearance of the images of black virgins and the cults of indigenous saints. For the landlords, these forms of syncretism served as stages of Christianization and were imposed on the slaves for social control and the submission of captives, as in most slave countries.

Since the colonial period, we have been in touch with the sacred in a very intimate and personal way. Saints and even Jesus were threatened or cursed if they did not respond to certain requests, and some of our older instincts arose. Examples include leaving an image of Saint Anthony hanging until a marriage was achieved, rubbing the image of a Saint to cure a sterile woman, or praying to Saint Longinus when searching for a lost object.

We were also strongly influenced by other European traditions, such as divination. An interesting example can be found in the 'Prayer of the Sieve and Scissors' to find thieves and stolen objects. This practice was documented in sixteenth-century England, Portugal, and Brazil.

Brazil also received visits from the Holy Inquisition, during which people were accused of witchcraft and several other heretical crimes. Many of the same European practices, ideas and images of witches were found here. Brazil even has some famous Portuguese sorceresses condemned to exile, like Antonia Maria, the sorceress of Beja. Brazilian witches and wizards - whether Europeans, Africans or natives - healed, made potions of love, conjured up various kinds of curses, provided protection, and even made deals with the devil, as in the European imagination. The only practice of European witchcraft that seems to lack any record for researchers in the area is the practice of sabbaths, which appeared to be more in the minds of inquisitors than in the practices of the damned.

Inquisition documents show that many of those accused of witchcraft in the colony - when taken to the Inquisition for interrogation and tortured - confessed to having participated in sabbaths in Val das Cavalinhas, a region famous for witchcraft in Portugal. This occurred even when they lived in Brazil or were newcomers from Africa.

It was within this religious context, diversified and coloured since colonial times by the passion of the Brazilians for magical and divinatory practices, that Wicca appeared and became popular in the country. The exact date the religion appeared in Brazil is not known, but at the end of the '80s, Farrar's book '*The Witches' God*' had been translated into Portuguese. The 90s brought a great interest in the subject with several other translations, including the famous book '*Brida*', by the Brazilian author Paulo Coelho, which tells the story of a young Irish woman in search of the path of magic, having as its master the character 'Wicca'. Through the movement created by Wicca, several other forms of paganism became known among

Brazilians. As the interest in Hekate and its cult is relatively recent in the country, and many of her devotees are young, most devotees I have contact with learned about Hekate through digital sources such as blogs or witchcraft communities. Unfortunately, much material produced in these spaces still portrays the image of Hekate as an old, shadowy and sometimes evil goddess, a 'dark' deity. But, increasingly, solid sources of information are coming to the knowledge of her devotees.

I am fascinated and intrigued by the incredible popularity of Hekate among Brazilians. Every time I get a chance to participate in pagan public events, I meet a large number of people who identify themselves as Hekate's children, which is also evident in the large number of Brazilian Facebook groups dedicated to Hekate (at least ten different ones to my knowledge) and a significant number of distinct groups of witchcraft linked to the Goddess in the country. From my point of view, what most of these devotees have in common is passionate and personal devotion, as is characteristic of Brazilian religiosity. Hekate is seen as a mother and protector for most of us, being present and active in our daily lives through dreams, meditations, messages and signs. Just as in colonial times, we tend to adapt the essence of what we resonate with to our practices without giving much importance to their formal or canonical study.

I believe Hekate is so popular among Brazilians because she continues to speak to those who walk through the threshold spaces and feel excluded from today's society. Hekate still has among her attributes the magic historically inherent in Brazilian religiosity, and she has become a deity somehow familiar to her Brazilian devotees.

Many Brazilian devotees are interested in studying the history of Hekate, its cult between the Greeks and their possible origins. But having the language as a barrier, and since few sources have been translated into Portuguese, in addition to the difficulty of access created by the high prices of imported books (often due to unfavourable exchange rates and long delivery times in the country) it is not surprising that formal knowledge about Hekate is not one of our best attributes.

Frustrated by the lack of scholarly sources for the study of Hekate a few of us got together to offer a solution. Reginaldo Rodrigues, Patricia Elizium and I created the *Sanctuary of Hekate Hegemonen* to focus on the research and analysis of the history of the Goddess in an attempt to make reliable information about Hekate accessible to the needs of modern Brazilian devotees. Our main activities include yearly free rituals open to the public. This includes the Rite of Her Sacred Fires[69] for which we typically host more than one hundred people. It is a beautiful and meaningful occasion to gather the community and have small lectures about her.

Our main offering is the *Circulo de Dadophoros*, a virtual and free-of-charge training program about Hekate. In November of 2023 we started our third class, with more than 250 enrolled participants. The program contains lectures about the Goddess' history and practical work through meditation. The program lasts 9 months, with monthly meetings and a mandatory reading list. Personally, facilitating this program has been a true blessing for me. The opportunity to teach about Hekate's history, accompany the students' development, and sharing in their personal stories is an integral part of my devotional practice.

We continue to encounter many different situations and needs that challenge our magical and personal skills and knowledge. For instance, we had students with several disabilities, post-traumatic stress disorder, depression and all manner of adverse circumstances in life, and seeing their effort and dedication to the Goddess is always deeply inspiring. Through the Circle, I had the privilege of helping two Brazilian history students find sources for researching Hekate. I hope that more

---

[69] Celebrated at the Full Moon of May.

Brazilian devotees will be writing academic material and devotional books about the Goddess in the coming years. And that some of our students will lead their own groups, developing and continuing to evolve Her devotion in this country.

Here, I should also highlight the importance of the Covenant of Hekate to make this possible. This free and open international organization enabled many of us to access knowledge and find devotees to connect with in our country. *The Circulo de Dadophoros* also prepared many Brazilians to join the Covenant of Hekate, especially those who were just beginning their practices. Many members even started learning English as a second language for the first time to learn more about Hekate. The importance and the love this Goddess inspires in her devotees are crystal clear.

The question *"Why Hekate?"* is asked frequently in the Brazilian pagan community and I don't pretend to know the answer. But it seems, to me at least, that there are many reasons why Brazilians love Hekate. She is a deity who speaks to those in need and those who feel excluded from our society, and Brazil is a country with vast social and economic inequality. Hekate has among her attributes many parallel magical practices historically inherent and familiar in Brazilian religiosity. She has transformed herself and her roles so many times during the ages that she became highly malleable, able to fit into almost any personal religious practice.

Above all, I think Hekate is a goddess that is somehow familiar to the Brazilian mind, not by history (of course!), but by fate.

BIBLIOGRAPHY

SOUZA, Laura de Mello e. The devil and the Land of Santa Cruz: witchcraft and popular religiosity in Colonial Brazil. São Paulo: Companhia das Letras, 2009

BEZERRA, Karina Oliveira. Wicca In Brazil: Magic, Adhesion and Permanence. São Paulo: Editorial Source, 2016

LANZA, A., & LAMOUNIER, M. Latin America as Destination of Immigrants: Brazil and Argentina (1870-1930). Cadernos PROLAM / USP, 14 (26), 90-107. Doi: http://dx.doi.org/10.11606/issn.1676-6288.prolam.2015.102283

Websites

http://www.slavevoyages.org/assessment/estimates

https://en.wikipedia.org/wiki/South_America

https://biblioteca.ibge.gov.br/visualizacao/periodicos/94/cd_2010_religiao_deficiencia.pdf

Hecate's Dreams & Oracles

Contributed by Carrie Kirkpatrick, London, UK

Hecate has long been associated with dreams, oracles and visions. In the ancient world, these were often regarded as direct messages from the divine. Oracles, specifically, are messages delivered through a priestess or priest who is in a semi-trance state and has usually had the deity invoked into them.

In ancient Greece, Oracles were very popular and an important part of day-to-day life, consulted regularly by people who sought answers to questions or messages from the deity to whom they were dedicated. The most famous oracle was Pythia, also known as the Oracle of Delphi, the temple was dedicated to the god Apollo but there's also evidence that it was dedicated to Themis before that.

Temple to Asteria on the Island of Delos, Greece

There was a widely held belief that there were 'good times and bad times' to approach the oracle. In Sicily in the 4th century CE, the oracle of Hecate said that the voice of the goddess was 'shut' because the planetary aspects were not compatible. I had my first experience of seeing an oracle through the priestess and co-founder of the Fellowship of Isis, Olivia Roberston. She lived in a beautifully magical and enchanting castle in Clonegal, Ireland called Huntingdon Castle and she turned the crypt into a massive temple dedicated to the goddess, creating shrines to different goddesses in every corner. Olivia gave me an oracle of the goddess Sekhmet, who would go on to be one of my main goddesses that I would work with in subsequent years.

Having trained as an Oracular Priestess within the Fellowship of Isis, I discovered that I had a natural affinity with this way of working. I had already been a professional psychic clairvoyant for many years and did possess some clairvoyant ability, however the experience of delivering an oracle of the goddess was different. I am aware of what I am saying when giving an oracle, but I have only a slight sense of what will be said before I say it. I understand the theme and the tone of the oracle, but do not steer the words. I have given oracles of goddesses that I am familiar with as well as those that I had not worked with before, and each time I was able to experience a strong connection. Although I seem to have a natural ability to give oracles, I am of the opinion that most people can achieve this, if they approach the goddess with a sincere heart. It is a skill that can be learned and practised.

Dreams were also regarded as significant messages from the divine in the ancient world, in particular they were described as coming directly from Hecate who was described as the *Source of Souls*. In the Chaldean Oracles it states, '*There is also a zone of dreams which has as its Origin the Source of Souls*'. Hecate's mother Asteria was also associated with dreams and believed to be the giver of dreams, and who delivered prophecies. Her temple at Delos was known as a temple of 'dream incubation', which is a thought technique whereby the person tries to make a specific dream happen in order to solve a problem. Therefore people would sleep in Asteria's temple with the intention of experiencing prophetic dreams, in the hope that they would receive answers to their problems.

You can practise dream incubation today and attempt to be aware that you are in a dream and direct your actions and reactions within the dream. Some simple techniques to practise are:

- Just before you go to sleep, write down the problem that you wish an answer to, keep it simple and as short as possible.
- Just before going to sleep, tell yourself that you want to dream an answer to your problem.

It is a good idea to keep a pen and paper by the bed so that you can write down the answer, or the first thing that comes to mind upon waking.

The ancient Greeks put great store in dream incubation and constructed many temples dedicated to Asclepius, the god of hospitals, which were called Asclepions. The most famous Asclepion was in Epidaurus; sick people would go to the temple and sleep there overnight in an attempt to be cured. Through dream incubation, they would hope to make contact with Asclepius via dreams. If they did dream of him, or if they dreamt they had been bitten by a snake, then this was regarded as confirmation that they had been visited by Asclepius and were cured. In many visual representations from that time, Asclepius is attended by one of his four daughters, Hygeia, the goddess of hygiene. Modern-day practitioners still call upon Asclepius and Hygeia to aid them in medical matters, and this was especially significant during the recent Covid pandemic. More in-depth rituals can also include Asclepius' other three daughters, Iaso – goddess of recuperation from illness, Aceso – goddess of the healing process and Panacea – goddess of universal remedy.

There were examples in the ancient world where people believed that dreams were direct messages from the gods and that they could also be prophetic or represent omens. Even in the Bible there were references to dream interpreters. Artemidorus of Daldis, who lived in the 2nd century CE, wrote a comprehensive text *Oneirocritica (The Interpretation of Dreams)*. Although Artemidorus believed that dreams could be prophetic and predict the future, he also paved the way for the modern approach to dream interpretation that we know today. He believed that the meaning of a dream image was not necessarily literal and that it could instead involve puns or symbols; these in turn could be understood by decoding the image into its component words. For example, Alexander the Great, while waging war against the Tyrians, dreamt that a satyr was dancing on his shield. Artemidorus reports that this dream was interpreted as follows: satyr = *sa tyros* ("Tyre will be thine"), predicting that Alexander would be triumphant.

As the ancient people clearly placed so much importance on dreams, as a mysterious connection with the divine or to have some otherworldly connection, it was not surprising that there were fears that evil forces could contact you through your dreams too, have access to your mind and maybe even attack you through your dreams. Early witch trials often cited dreams as a form of attack by a witch on a poor unsuspecting soul. Both dreams and nightmares were associated with Hecate as it was believed that she could send both, depending upon whether you had offended her or pleased her. In the 5th century BCE, Hippocrates wrote:

> *'If the patient is attended by fears, terrors, and madness in the night, jumps up out of his bed and flees outside, they call these the attacks of Hecate or the onslaughts of ghosts...'*

This brings us to sleep paralysis, which is a relatively new term to describe what for hundreds of years many believed to be a visitation by a malevolent creature which attacked its victims as they slept. Different cultures have different explanations for sleep paralysis demons. The Canadian Inuit attribute the sleep paralysis to spells of shamans whilst Japanese folklore says it is a vengeful spirit that suffocates its enemies in their sleep. And the Mara demons were feminine nightmare spirits found in Slavic and Teutonic mare mythology. The Slavic words *mora*, *morava*, and *zmora* have their roots in the Greek word *moros*, which means death. For the Croats, mora means 'nightmare', but it also refers to a succubus, a demonic entity that visited men in their dreams and tormented them with longing. The concept is that these were feminine spirits that intentionally tangled men's hair in their sleep to give them 'mare-locks,' 'mare-braids,' and 'mare-tangles.' Old Norse legend tells of a mara that would slither into a bedroom at night, hover on top of a sleeping person, and inflict nightmares. Usually, the victim would become paralyzed when the mare visited and felt a heavy weight starting at the foot but ending on the chest, leaving the victim feeling suffocated, panicked, and breathless.

In Scandinavian folklore, sleep paralysis is caused by a *Mare*, a supernatural creature related to incubi and succubi. The mare is a damned woman, who is cursed and her body is carried mysteriously during sleep and without her noticing. In Iceland folk culture sleep paralysis is generally called having a *Mara*. A goblin or a succubus (since it is generally female) is believed to cause nightmares (the origin of the word 'nightmare' itself is derived from an English cognate of her name).

The truth behind sleep paralysis is that during REM sleep, your body is relaxed and your muscles don't move. Sleep paralysis occurs when the sleep cycle is shifting between stages. When you wake up suddenly from REM, your brain is awake, but your body is still in REM mode and can't move, causing you to feel like you're paralyzed.

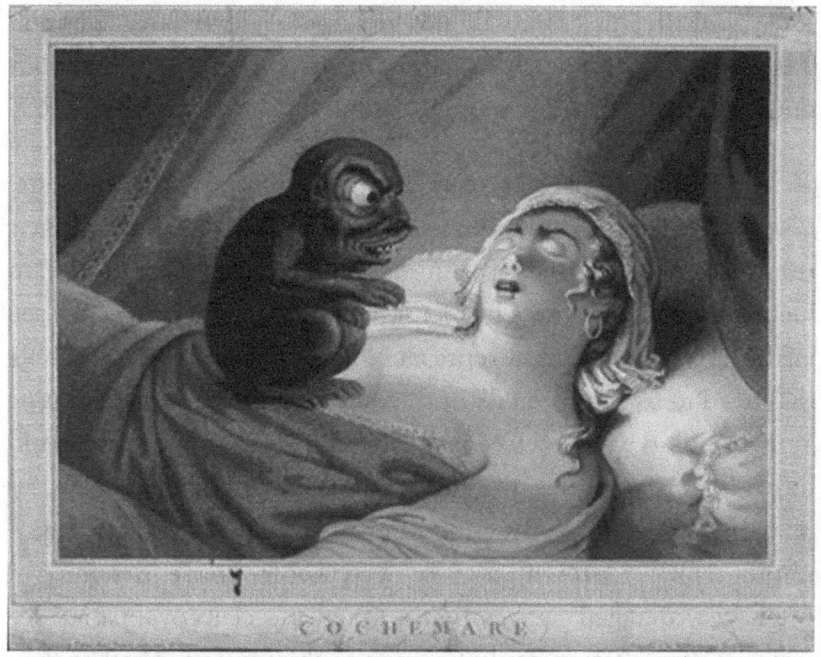

Cochemare (Nightmare) by Jean Pierre Simon, 1810, depicting an incubus perched upon the bare breast of a woman being provoked into a terrifying dream.

As we feel at our most vulnerable when asleep, and we generally regard the dream realm as an otherworld, the concept that we could be subject to attack during our sleep has endured and formed the basis of many horror films today. We continue to be fascinated by the otherworldly realm of dreams and the parts of the mind that we do not necessarily feel in control of. Dreams have continued to fascinate us throughout the ages and over time they ceased to be the realm solely of the Divine and started to become messages from deep within ourselves. At the end of the 19th century, dreams became regarded more as messages from our unconscious, and psychoanalysts would interpret them as a way to unravel the psychological troubles of their patients. The emergence of New Age spiritual practices saw dreams become gateways to our souls and people set up in practice offering their skills in dream interpretation, as a method of problem-solving and self-development for their clients. So, for magical practitioners today, our dreams could fall into any one of these categories and it is up to us to decide what kind of dream it is before we set about understanding what it is trying to tell us.

Some of us remember our dreams, some of us don't. Some keep a diary, some don't. Some try to control and influence their responses to what is happening in their dreams through dream incubation, whilst others just let it happen. Are the images we see in the dream state literal representations or metaphors, symbols that need to be interpreted? Both could be true, we may not know at the time, so we need to consider both options. The same could be said of clairvoyance, the ability to see with your mind's eye, an image which you can describe in great detail. But is the image a photographic representation or a symbol? Those fleeting yet often very detailed images that a practising clairvoyant may see during a consultation could be open to interpretation rather than just taken at face value.

EXAMPLE DREAM

In my friend, a Hekate Priestess' dream, she was standing with her son on the bank of a river at night and saw a friend of mine, whom we shall call Jay, as the ferryman Charon, coming towards her across the River Styx on his boat. She wondered if he was coming for her, but he said no, he was here for someone else and sailed past. When she awoke, she wondered if this was a portent and that someone she knew might die.

My friend Jay later told me that they had come across an old acquaintance in the street just the day before, and that this person had been in a bad way, very drunk and sitting on the side of the pavement, very distressed and unable to get themselves home. Jay remembered this man from many years ago and stopped to help him. He supported the man on his shoulder and took him home to his flat, which was up several flights of stairs. When inside Jay helped him into his bed and the man, barely coherent, kept repeating 'Oh God, thank you.'

It was two weeks later that Jay heard that this man had passed away and after making some enquiries, he realised that he had died on the same day that Jay had taken him home. It transpired that he had been the last person to see him alive and had enabled him to die peacefully in his own bed.

Jay had embarked upon a study of Hecate a few months before this happened and I saw immediately that this was the influence of the goddess inspiring him to help this man to cross over safely and not alone in the gutter.

So this shows us that dreams can be portents, we don't necessarily get to act on them but in this case a priestess of Hecate was alerted to the role that Jay would be playing in the near future.

Now I come onto a different kind of dream, I am talking about the dreams that we have, our hopes, our passions, our aspirations of what we would like to achieve in our lives. How many of you have abandoned your dreams because you changed your mind or your life took on a new direction? How many of you are still holding onto your dreams secretly hoping that one day you may get a chance to realise them? In today's world, we are not encouraged to follow our dreams. Life can be challenging and we are expected to just accept it and be more realistic in our expectations. This could be sound and grounded advice, but not in every case. I would like to ask you to revisit or reconsider some of your dreams.

We will take a guided journey to a cave of dreams where you will have the opportunity to rekindle an old dream or maybe embrace a new one. During this pathworking you will be asked to visualise images. Now not everyone can naturally form images in their mind. It doesn't matter, some people are naturally very visual and some aren't. However, if your intention is clear, then you will achieve the desired results regardless of whether you can see images with your mind or not. I am inviting you to bypass the limiting belief that says 'I can't' when it comes to visualising your dreams. It is not an order, but rather a suggestion. I would like you to 'pretend' that you are visualising. You may choose to focus on key words or elements of your intention, you may want to see yourself smiling and feeling confident that you are doing it successfully. Your mind may throw up another idea to help you with the process, but the end result is that you will be able to visualise your chosen dream.

PATHWORKING

Close your eyes, take a few deep breaths, and imagine the earth beneath your feet, the pulsing green energy of the earth coming up through your feet, up your legs, your pelvis though your base chakra and up to the sacral chakra and the solar plexus, then passing through the solar plexus it loops back down to the earth, a pulsing green loop of earth energy grounding you.

Now see a golden ball of light above your head, your inner wisdom and spirit passing through your crown chakra, third eye, heart chakra and solar plexus, touching the loop of earth energy, passing through your solar plexus and up past your back forming a loop of golden energy, connecting you to your true authentic energy.

Now I would like you to see yourself walking through a woodland, it is nearly dark and you can just see the path ahead of you. You follow it through the trees until you come to a rocky hillside and there you can see an opening in the side of the rockface. You enter into the opening and see two flaming torches on the walls, illuminating the way ahead. If you wish, you may take a torch and carry it with you. You follow the path until it leads you into a cave with flaming torches on the walls. In the centre of the cave is a pool of water, deep and still. Beyond the pool is an opening, you hear a rustling noise and emerging from the shadows is the goddess Hecate. She may appear to you in her triple form or as a single form. She may be accompanied by her totem animals, the snake, the dog, the bull, the lion, the horse. She may be holding her symbols, the key, the knife, the cord. As she emerges from the opening, she picks up two flaming torches from the wall and steps towards you, standing on the other side of the pool of water.

She welcomes you and explains that as you meet her in her domain, you may choose to change the path that you follow in your life, if you so wish. You may revisit your dreams or create new ones, go beyond the limits of your imagination and dare to dream in the material world. She holds her torches before her, illuminating the water in the deep dark pool. At first you see your own reflection in the water, the goddess stoops down and disturbs the surface of the water.

What do you see? After a few moments look back up to the goddess and she may speak to you, or give you something. Ask her a question if you wish.

When you feel ready, thank the goddess and take your leave from the cave, safe in the knowledge that you can return at any time. Come back through the tunnel and out into the woodland and back from whence you came. When you are ready, bring your awareness back into the room, wiggle your toes, gently move your arms and your legs and then open your eyes.

Watch Carrie Kirkpatrick's tribute to Olivia Robertson at the following YouTube link:
https://www.youtube.com/watch?v=CSO0go533Go

The Lamia:
Followers of Hekate

Contributed by Hazel, Yorkshire UK

The Lamia as a group or as an individual is known as a creature that feeds from babies and men providing the inspiration for the vampire/succubus. The Lamia is portrayed as a half-woman half snake and has become closely associated with Hecate, even referred to as the children of Hecate who travelled in her wake (Atsma, 2011) similar to the Empousae.

Interestingly, the Lamia and Hecate are also linked in different versions of myths, in as much that they are both referred to as Scylla's mother with the use of the epithet *Krataiis*[70]. Additionally, West (1990) suggests that both Hecate and Lamia evolved from the Mesopotamian demon Lamashtu. Understanding the Lamia requires going back in time to study her roots.

ORIGINS

The origins of the Lamia begin with Lamassu who was a Sumerian kind and helpful wind-spirit commonly erected as a protective statue by Kings. The Sumerians inhabited South Mesopotamia (modern-day Iraq and Northern Kuwait) during the Early Bronze Age (Kriwaczek, 2010) before the rise of the Minoan civilisation in Greece circa 2050 BCE. As newcomers, and their religions appropriating characters from old religions into demons in an attempt to stigmatise them (Eisler, 1987), the Akkadians from circa 2300-2200 BCE transformed the Sumerian

---

[70] (see Pausanias [2nd c. CE] Description of Greece and Stesichorus [7-6th c. BCE] for reference to Lamia as Scylla's mother and Apollonius Rhodius' [3rd c. BCE] Argonautica for reference to Hecate as her mother [Atsma, 2011])

Lamassu into Lamashtu, daughter of the God of Heaven Anû, who was also seen as the precursor to Lilith (Hurwitz, 2009).

Lamashtu thus became a blood-sucking creature watching over pregnant women with the intention of feeding on their babies. She is viewed as the personification of a disease that only afflicts children. As a wind-spirit, she is associated with birds of prey amongst other animals; lionesses, wolves, donkeys, snakes, pigs, and dogs, and is commonly depicted with these animals in different hybrid forms (West, 1990; Hurwitz, 2009).

Archaeological evidence has revealed a considerable number of amulets and texts employed to be rid of her (West, 1990; Burkert, 1995), one of which has specific symbolic elements linked to Hecate: Lamashtu is given food, a pair of sandals and sacrificial dogs to help her in her journey away from a household. As West (1990) describes, Lamashtu has come to be seen as a canine Goddess with a particular interest in puppies. A lot of the information on Lamashtu has come from the common Babylonian text Labartu, which was translated by D.W. Myhrman in 1902. The reason for the difference between the names Lamashtu and Labartu came from a mistranslation of the cuneiform symbols for mas̆ and bar which looked identical (Burkert, 1995; Hurwitz, 2009).

As the Minoan culture rose from circa 2000 BCE and eventually the Mycenaean from 1650 BCE during the Old Babylonian Period, extensive trade between the East and Greece permitted religious artefacts and deities to migrate into Greece. West (1990) describes extensively archaeological and linguistic evidence that indicate without doubt that such migrations heavily influenced the Ancient Greek religion. Ultimately, Lamashtu entered into the Greek pantheon as the Lamia, where the name Lamia originated from the Greek term laimos, meaning jaws (West, 1990; Burkert, 1995; Hurwitz, 2009).

THE LAMIA IN GREEK RELIGION

The Lamia as the Shark

The first source referring to the Lamia was by Stesichorus in the Archaic Age sometime between 750-550 BCE which is around and a little after Hesiod and his Theogeny mentioning Hecate. In this early source, Lamia is the daughter of Scylla, representing her as a shark. This is one of two myths where she is the daughter of Poseidon. Stesichorus explains that she had Scylla with Phorkys (Atsma, 2011) while Pausanias much later in his 'Description of Greece', outlines that Lamia, with Zeus, had a son: Akheilos (the lipless one who was eventually cursed by Aphrodite to be ugly), and the Sibyl Hierophile who gave oracles at a temple associated with oceanic deities. Lamia as a shark has also been mentioned in later sources: Ptolemy Hephaistion in New History (1st to 2nd century CE), Photius in Myriobiblon (9th century CE) and Eustathius in Homer's Odyssey (1115-1195 CE) (Atsma, 2011). Instinctively the meaning behind her name i.e. 'jaws', gives reference to her as a predator and thus her name has inspired the nomenclature of a family of sharks, the Lamnidae.

Queen of Libya

The most well-known myth of the Lamia is where she is the beautiful Queen of Libya, daughter of Belus/Belos with whom Zeus had an affair. Hera found out about the affair and, while in some versions she stole or killed Lamia's children, in another account she drove Lamia to kill her own children. Her distress at having lost her children drove Lamia crazy with grief. In some versions her grief is what turned her into a monster, while in others it was her raging revenge on killing others' children (Atsma, 2011) that deformed her. In all versions, Lamia was said to be cursed so as never to be able to sleep. However, Zeus, taking pity on her, gave her the ability to remove her eyes so that she could (Helmbod, 1939). This version of Lamia as the Queen of

Libya first appeared in the literature Libyan Histories by Duris of Samos 380-310 BCE (Whitehead and Roth, 2014) at the start of the Hellenistic Period. This reference by Duris of Samos was later used by Diodorus Siculus (1st century BCE) and later referred to by Aelius Aristides in his Panathenaicus between 171-181 CE (West, 1990).

Mountainous Beast

This myth of the Lamia encompasses an individual who is more beast-like. In this version the Lamia still has her origins in Libya as Queen and she feeds from babies and children, which was used to hold children accountable for their behaviour, as Strabo (64-21 BCE) writes in his Geography (Jones, 1917). She is also known to be particularly hideous and even smelly, as some some scholiasts of the 19th and 20th centuries on Aristophanes' writings suggest, referring to The Wasps and Peace (West, 1990), and she lives in a cave. In a way, this version is almost an additional aspect to her as Queen of Libya, but the emphasis is placed on her savagery and her habitation in the mountains. This version is first directly referred to in Strabo's Geography (Jones, 1917) where she lives near where she was born in Automala in Libya. Dio Chrysostom (1st century CE) in his Fifth Discourse (Cohoon, 1939) also refers to this adaptation and describes her as a half woman and half snake, and Antoninus Liberalis (2nd century CE) places the Lamia in Mount Kirphis in Parnassos near Delphi. Liberalis cites a story about how a youth was sent as a sacrifice for the monster, but upon meeting a group of men, one of the group, named Eurybatis, falls in love with the youth and offers himself up as a sacrifice instead. He finds Lamia and eventually kills her by throwing her off the edge of a cliff (West, 1990).

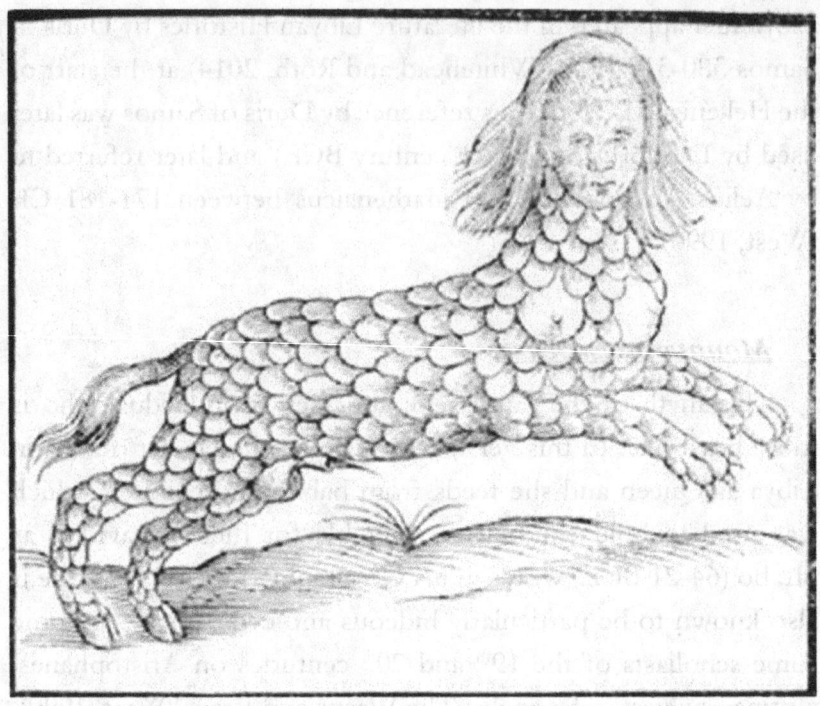

Topsell, E. 1658. *The History of Four-footed Beasts and Serpents.*
London: E. Cotes for G. Sawbridge

<u>Vampire Femme-fatale</u>

Eventually the myth further evolved to make Lamia into a kind of ghoul. This adaptation focuses on blood-sucking and the seduction of young men, leaving out entirely babies and children as a source of nourishment for her. She loses her beast-like quality and instead of being one individual, becomes known as a species or class of demon. This scenario has a unique motif: a young woman who is Lamia finds and seduces a young man to use as her continuous food source. Because this type of Lamia has magical abilities, she uses them to deceive the young man. Eventually, she is discovered by another character within the narrative who points it out to the victim, causing her to flee. This version first appeared in Plutarch (45-120 CE) in 'The Parallel Lives' as a story of The Life of Demetrius (Perrin, 1919) where

Demetrius is the victim and King Lysimachus is the one to 'out' her.

A particularly well-known story of the Lamia is in the 'Life of Apollonius of Tyana' by Flavius Philostratus (170-247 CE) which centres on a Corinthian Lamia. Here, Menippus is the victim and is one of Apollonius' students (Conybeare, 1912). Eusebius' (4th century CE) treatment of the subject of the Lamia in his 'Treatise Against Hierocles' remains as a reply to Philostratus (Atsma, 2011). Phlegan of Tralles (2nd century CE) recites a narrative in the Book of Marvels which Proclus (5th century CE) picks up on; Phillinon died as an unwed maiden and upon returning to her home sees and falls in love with a guest there, Makhates, whom she tries to seduce. Once seen by her mother however she falls back dead.

CHARACTER

To understand (the) Lamia, we have to look at the running themes throughout all the myths.

The first theme is her choice of victims. From her origins as Lamashtu, her primary victims are children. She was responsible for the death of new-born and stillborn babies, and amulets and protective spells were used to keep her away to ensure infant survival (Burkert, 1995; West, 1990). Attacking babies and children clearly became a prevalent theme for the most common version of the myth featuring Zeus and Hera. By going against the very nature of what being a woman in the ancient world meant - namely to breed, she is seen as infertile, maybe even a hermaphrodite and thus cast out and stigmatised by society (Johnston, 1999). Her monstrosity is capitalised upon to make children behave themselves (Jones, 1917). This is in stark contrast to Hecate and in particular her *Kourotrophos* aspect, as Hecate watches over babies and pregnant women (Von Rudloff, 1999). Additionally, this does complement how Lamia could potentially come to be under Hecate's remit, as Hecate is associated with outcasts. The notion of the Lamia as infertile hags and becoming associated with witches (who were also seen to come under Hecate's remit) is a notable aspect in the story *The Golden Ass* by Apuleius (2nd century CE) (Leinweber, 1994).

Her second type of victim are men, which is first mentioned by Dio Chrysostom in 1st century CE (Cohoon, 1939) although he does not mention why. Signs of the femme fatale/succubus start to come through:

> "... the face was that of a woman...the breast and bosom, and the neck too, were extremely beautiful...the complexion was of dazzling brightness, the glance of the eyes aroused affection and yearning in the souls of all that beheld." Cohoon (1939)

Her beauty as Queen of Libya whom Zeus lusts after may have had some bearing on her femme fatale nature. In other words, just as Hera punishes her for Zeus's actions, Lamia becomes the one to blame for leading men (and Zeus) astray, thereby should a man encounter Lamia he is not held accountable for acting on his desires. This femme fatale evolves in later texts to become less savage (i.e. living in a cave) to be more vampiric, an individual who walks in the cities amongst people and is able to deceive them with magical powers, such as written by Plutarch (Perrin, 1919), Philostratus (Conybeare, 1912) and Phlegan of Tralles (Atsma, 2011). As with both Lamia's and Lamashtu's victims, the modus operandi is however the same; they suck blood and feast upon flesh thus representing the earliest vampire form as well as the succubus (once men are eventually included as a food group). Her role as a shark and mother of Scylla certainly suggests that it may have lent itself to her modus operandi, notably that she attacks and destroys with teeth and jaws.

The second concurrent theme lies in her mythical origins. In almost all versions save for when Lamia is referred to as a race, she is from Libya. Her father's name Belos or Belus is a

Hellenised version of Baal providing distinct evidence that she is a foreigner (Johnston, 1999) and has been described as black (Johnston, 1999 and Seltman, 1920).

Painted vase depicting Lamia being tortured by five satyrs, 5th cemtury B.C.E. De Agostini Picture Library / M. Carrieri / Bridgeman Images

Different versions of the Lamia myth place Belus/Belos in different locales. Nevertheless, the common theme is that she comes from the "barbarian" world which further contributes to her "monster" status. This certainly fits with her archaeological and historical origins from the Lamashtu further East.

The final theme is the change from the individual Lamia to the race of creatures Lamiae. This starts with Plutarch in The Parallel Lives (Perrin, 1919) where a Lamia is a vampiric woman returned from the dead as opposed to an already living beast. This change from singular to plural could reference the fact that any young woman could return from the dead with the same feeding habits as the individual Lamia thus designating a new class of demons. Once the Lamiae have become a race of demons, their similar habits to the Empousae (targeting men) would entail their association to Hecate. However, even as an individual she joins the company of the Empousae (Graves, 1992). As one author describes in West (1990), most of the demons/monsters associated with Hecate (Empousae, Mormo, and Lamia) can be merged into one another.

DISCUSSION

The Lamia has undergone a few transformations since she entered into the Greek pantheon most likely during Minoan culture from 2050 BCE due to religious migration from the East. She has evolved from the personification of a disease that inflicts only children to a seductive femme fatale providing the foundation for vampires. Having said that, how and why she added young men to her prey remains to be seen. It may be linked to the most common myth that she was once a beautiful Queen. Her association with snakes is also open to debate, but snakes could be also associated with other Mesopotamian female demons from which other Greek creatures may originate. West (1990) does suggest that Hecate, Lamia, the Gorgon and Scylla all have origins in Lamashtu, even though he largely bases his connection between Hecate and Lamashtu on Hecate's 'darker' aspects.

Lamia and Hecate do share many features: both are said to be Scylla's mother in different myths, babies and children feature highly, snakes are significant animals in their symbolism, they both exist as representatives of outcasts and between the liminal space of the dead and the living, and they both have possible similar origins in the East. While Hecate has many other aspects to her that do not overlap with the Lamia, the considerable associations between the two do beg the question: could these similarities be the reason for Lamia becoming Hecate's followers?

Perhaps it is, even though the reason is never specifically stated in any source, only that the Lamia eventually became associated with Hecate (Atsma, 2011; Graves, 1992). Deities and mythical creatures can evolve from the same roots, and associations between the end-points of such evolution could be the very reason that deities and creatures merge (Fox, 2008).

Nevertheless, the Lamia, whether on her own or with Hecate, has proved to be a complex character that has had significant effects even in recent times. John Keats was inspired to write his lengthy poem on her (Keats, 1820) and she has made her way into pop culture and continues to this day to influence the horror genre.

REFERENCES

Atsma, A.J., 2000-2011. The Theoi Project. Available from: http://www.theoi.com/

Burkert, W. 1995. The Orientalizing Revolution: Near- Eastern Influence on Greek Culture in the Early Archaic Age. Translated by Pinder, M.E. and Burkert, W. Harvard University Press, USA.

Cohoon, J.W. (trans.) 1939. Discourses by Dio Chrysotom. Loeb Classical Library 339. Reproduced *The Fifth Discourse* and available at: http://penelope.uchicago.edu/Thayer/E/Roman/Texts/Dio_Chrysostom/Discourses/5*.html Accessed: October 2014

Conybeare, F.C. (trans.) 1912. The Life of Apollonius of Tyana, by Philostratus. From Hare, J.B. 1999. Internet Sacred Text Archive. Available at: http://www.sacred-texts.com/cla/aot/laot/laot20.htm Accessed: 28/07/2014.

Eisler, R. 1987. The Chalice and the Blade. Harper and Row Publishers.

Fox, R.L. 2008. Travelling Heroes: Greeks and their Myths in the Epic Age of Homer. Penguin Books, UK.

Graves, R. 1992. The Greek Myths (Complete Edition). Penguin Books, London.

Helmbod, W.C. (trans.) 1939. Moralia by Plutarch Volume 6. Loeb Classical Library 337. Reproduced *On being a busybody* and available at: http://penelope.uchicago.edu/Thayer/E/Roman/Texts/Plutarch/Moralia/De_curiositate*.html Accessed: October 2014

Hurwitz, S. 2009. Lilith: The First Eve 3rd Edition. Daimon Verlag, Switzerland.

Johnston, S. I.1990. Restless Dead: Encounters between the Living and the Dead in Ancient Greece. University of California Press, USA.

Jones, H.L. (trans.) 1917. Geography by Strabo. Loeb Classical Library 267, Book 17. Reproduced Book 1, Chapter 2 available at: http://penelope.uchicago.edu/Thayer/E/Roman/Texts/Strabo/1B1*.html

Accessed: October 2014

Keats, J. 1820. Lamia. The Online Literature Network, Jalic Inc. Publishers. Available at: http://www.online-literature.com/poe/2055/

Kriwaczek, P. 2010. Babylon: Mesopotamia and The Birth of Civilization. Atlantic Books, UK.

Leinweber, D.W. 1994. Witchcraft and Lamiae in "The Golden Ass". Folklore 105, 77-82.

Perrin, B. (trans.) 1919. Lives by Plutarch Volume 9. Loeb Classical Library 101, Reproduced *The Life of Demetrius* and available at: http://penelope.uchicago.edu/Thayer/E/Roman/Texts/Plutarch/Lives/Demetrius*.html

Accessed: October 2014

Von Rudloff, R. 1999. Hekate in Ancient Greek Religion. Horned Owl Publishing, Canada.

Seltman, C.T. 1920. Two Heads of Negresses. American Journal of Archaeology 24 (1), 14-26.

Topsell, E. 1658. *The History of Four-footed Beasts and Serpents*. London: E. Cotes for G. Sawbridge

West, D.R 1990. Some Cults of Greek Goddesses and Female Daemons of Oriental Origins especially in relation to the mythology of goddesses and daemons in the Semitic world. PhD Thesis. University of Glasgow.

Whitehead, D and Roth, C. 2014. SUDA online entry lambda 84: Lamia. Available at: http://www.stoa.org/sol-entries/lambda/84 Accessed: 04/08/14

Searching for Lamia

Contributed by Lyza, Yorkshire UK

Photo by James Lacey of Dark Soul Photography

Gothla, the UK's premier gothic belly dance event (www.gothla.co.uk) is an event dear to me, since I first began performing on their open stage in 2008. So, when their organisers asked me to perform and teach at their next show in 2014, I was both excited and daunted by the task. Luckily, I had already planned a visit to Greece with Hazel for two weeks in August 2013. Hazel and I chatted for hours, went to the museums, and I read Daniel Ogden's 'Night's Black Agents: Witches, Wizards and the Dead in the Ancient World' on the beach - and all the other usual holiday activities. So this, mixed in with Hazel's research and my meditation and dance work over the next year, led to my performance at Gothla in July 2014.

Lamia as an individual is an intricate character with various, sometimes contradictory, backstories and histories. She is often portrayed as half snake and half woman in ancient Greece, but more commonly as a woman with magical abilities who lures, traps, and devours men. Although dressing myself up as half snake or as a shark could have potential as a fun, comedy performance in the future, I decided to approach Lamia as a woman with magical abilities (it was also kinder on my bank balance).

Looking at her as a more human character made her far more appealing to me, as she immediately had more depth as a character as well. *'Lamiae exist in a poignantly tragic condition: they are forever destined to kill and eat the men with whom they fall in love.'* (page 164, Ogden, 2008). To me, this seemed to link very well to the myth of Lamia as the Queen of Libya and the brutal punishment inflicted upon her by Hera. Her family is killed, or Lamia herself is compelled to kill them, and she is also turned into a monster who is fated to kill anyone she may ever love again. A story far more interesting than the standard vampire femme-fatale, her actions as a 'monster' come from a place of deep pain and torment, whether those actions are forced or her own.

Then my search for Lamia took an interesting turn on Facebook. After sharing some promo shots, Katerina told me that she had read that the Lamia only visited men who were guilty of adultery. I loved this, as it almost begins to empower Lamia again, making her a vengeful figure. Once I learned this, her story for me came together with an overarching theme: 'evil is made not born'.

Then a good friend and costume designer made my costume in the photos you see. Organic Armour made the Grecian Tiara and armbands which were inspired by the statues I saw in various museums in Greece. I pulled together a mix of music that fitted the story I wanted to tell and spent months choreographing Lamia, starting with meeting her after Hera's curse dealing with the pain and loss, the torment driving her to madness. Then we see her becoming the Lamia we know from myth. A monster, but one who only kills men who are adulterers. After all, why is it always the women's fault?

Photo by Sue Hutton, SoozVyooz

With thanks to the Gothla team, Endenisia my costume designer, Organic Armour, my dance friends and teachers, Sword-Swinging Robot, Dark Soul Photography, Soozvyooz, Katerina, Hazel, and Leo.

References

Ogden, D. (2008) Night's Black Agents: Witches, Wizards, and the Dead in the Ancient

World. Continuum Books.

The Ephesian Letters

Contributed by Sorita d'Este, Glastonbury, UK

One of the oldest and most significant sets of voces magicae (a term used for magical words of unknown meaning and origin) was the Ephesian Letters or Characters, a group of six words. These words were askion, kataskion, lix, tetrax, damnameneus AND aision (or aisia). We cannot be absolutely certain whether the Ephesian Letters were specifically connected with Hekate, though from the evidence it does seem likely. Their first known appearance was in a Mycenaean inscription from the 5th century BCE.

The Ephesian Letters occur a number of times in the Greek Magical Papyri in charms which call on Hekate (Betz, 1996). Thus, the first two of the Ephesian Letters were used in a Hekate charm associated with initiation (PGM LXX.12) as part of a string of voces magicae being:

'Askei Kataskei Eron Oreon Ior Mega Samnyer Baui Phobantia Semne.'

The fifth word, damnameneia, was used in the Bear Charm, which included a reference to Hekate as Brimo (PGM VII. 686-702). A 2nd to the 3rd century CE lead defixion tablet to Hekate as torch bearer of the crossroads also uses this word repeatedly (SM 49) (Betz, 1996).

An early fragmentary protective charm on a lead tablet from Phalasarna on Crete included the Ephesian Letters with phrases indicative of a Hekate-like 'She-wolf'. It is also interesting to note that they are called the Orphic Formula in the Greek Magical Papyri (PGM VII. 451) (Betz, 1996). Considering the connections between Hekate and the Orphic Mysteries this is another hint which suggests a specific ritual connection with Hekate and these words.

The Ephesian Letters were also referred to by the Greek poet Anaxilas in his lost 4th-century BCE play The Harp Maker when he wrote '[unnamed person] *carries around marvellous Ephesian letters in sewn pouches.*' Various qualities were attributed to the Ephesian Letters, including endowing the wearer with great power (particularly wrestlers as described in Eustathius, Photius and the Suda) and protecting newly married couples (mentioned by Menander, fragment 371).

It should also be noted that when Plutarch commented on the powers of the Ephesian Letters (Moralia 706E), he referred to daimones who were specifically under the rule of Hekate:

> *'For just as sorcerers advise those possessed by daimones to recite and name over to themselves the Ephesian letters.'*

The Christian theologian Clement of Alexandria, who was well known for being the teacher of the theologian Origen, recorded suggested meanings for the Ephesian Letters in his work Stromata (Miscellanies) in the early 3rd century CE:

> *'Androkydes the Pythagorean, indeed, says that the so-called Ephesian letters, which were well-known among many, were of the order of symbols. And he said that Askion is darkness, for this has no shadow; and Kataskion is light, since it casts a shadow with its rays; and Lix is the earth, according to the ancient name; and Tetrax is the year, according to the seasons; and Damnameneus is the sun, the tamer; and Aisia is the true word. And truly the symbol signifies that the divine things have been set in order: darkness to light, the sun to the year, the earth to every kind of genesis of nature.*[71]*'*

Returning to the words used in the Rite of Her Sacred Fires, 'Askei Kataskei Eron Oreon Ior Mega Samnyer Baui Phobantia Semne', as voces magicae we cannot know for certain what they

---

[71] d'Este & Rankine, 2009, pg 65-69

meant or when they were used, but we can draw together likely speculations. From Clement of Alexandria we can see that the phrase starts with Askei Kataskei which could mean 'darkness, light'. Mega in Greek means 'great', and it has been suggested that Baui may refer to the barking of a dog (Betz 1996, pg. 297, fn. 7). All these speculations hint at Hekate's associations with both darkness and light, greatness and dogs. As such, it is possible that this phrase was a coded sequence which called on Hekate's powers.

Today, the Ephesian letters continue to be used in rites honouring Hekate. It is being used to honour Her, and also to protect and empower other types of magical rites.

References

Betz, H-D, ed. 1996. The Greek Magical Papyri in Translation. Chicago: University of Chicago Press.

d'Este, S. and Rankine, D. 2009. Hekate: Liminal Rites. London: Avalonia.

The Orphic Hymn to Hekate

Contributed by James Van Kollenburg (Kallimakhos)

It is significant that the Orphic hymns open with the hymn to Hekate; (Gr. Ἑκάτη). She is found in the Orphǽohs Argonaftiká (Ὀρφέως Ἀργοναυτικά); Orphéfs (Ὀρφε) invokes her in order to gain entry into the grove that harbours the Krysómallon Dǽras (ὑςΧρυσόμαλλον Δέρας), the Golden Fleece. She is also found in the mythology of Dimítir (Δημήτηρ) as she seeks out her daughter in the great story connected with the most famous of all the Mystery cults, the Ælefsínia Mystíria (Ἐλευσίνια Μυστήρια), for Ækáti has heard the cries of Pærsæphóni (Περσεφόνη) as she was abducted by Ploutohn (Πλούτων). And Isíodos (Hesiod; Gr. Ἡσίοδος) in his *Theogonía* (Θεογονία) 410-452 says that Zefs (Ζεύς) reveres (τίμησε) her above all and that she is greatly honoured by all the Deathless Gods in Starry Heaven (ἀστερόεντος ἀπ' οὐρανοῦ); the poem goes on to enumerate many benefits the Goddess bestows on people. It is said that Ækáti holds the hands of those who pray and that she takes particular notice of those people who wish to develop Virtue (Ἀρετή).

So, who is this mighty goddess? Perhaps her hymn will provide us with some clues to understanding her and getting closer to her.

<u>*Original Greek Text:*</u>

1. Ὕμνος εις Ἑκάτην.
Εἰνοδίην Ἑκάτην κλῄιζω, τριοδῖτιν, ἐραννήν, 1
οὐρανίην, χθονίαν τε, καὶ εἰναλίην κροκόπεπλον,
τυμβιδίην, ψυχαῖς νεκύων μέτα βακχεύουσαν,
Πέρσειαν, φιλέρημον, ἀγαλλομένην ἐλάφοισιν,

νυκτερίην, σκυλακῖτιν, ἀμαιμάκετον βασίλειαν, 5
ταυροπόλον, παντὸς κόσμου κληιδοῦχον ἄνασσαν,
ἡγεμόνην, νύμφην, κουροτρόφον, οὐρεσιφοῖτιν,
λισσομένοις κούρην τελεταῖς ὁσίαισι παρεῖναι
βουκόλῳ εὐμενέουσαν ἀεὶ κεχαρηότι θυμῷ.

Reuchlinian transliteration of the ancient Greek text:

Einodíin Ækátin klíizoh, triodítin, ærannín, 1
ouraníin, khthonían tæ, kai einalíin, krokópæplon,
tymvidíin, psykhais nækýohn mǽta vakkhévousan,
Pǽrseian, philǽrimon, agallomǽnin ælaphisin,
nyktæríin, skylakítin, amaimákæton vasíleian, 5
tavropólon, pandós kózmou kliidoukhon ánassan,
iyæmónin, nýmphin, kourotróphon, ouræsiphítin,
lissómænis kourin tælætais osíaisi pareinai
voukólo evmænæousan aei kækharióti thymó.

Breakdown of the Hymn

Ὕμνος (hymn) εἰς (to) Ἑκάτην (Ækáti)

Εἰνοδίην (crossroads) Ἑκάτην (Ækáti) κλῄζω (call) - *I call Ækáti of the crossroads*. Εἰνοδίην (fem. acc.) is a form of εἰνοδία (fem. nom.) or ἐνόδιος (masc. nom), a common epithet of the Goddess meaning 'of the crossroads'. And κλῄζω is a form of κλύω, 'hear' 'listen'.

τριοδῖτιν - Ækáti is τριοδῖτις (fem. nom.; τριοδίτης is masc. nom.), worshipped at the meeting of three roads.

ἐραννήν – Fem. acc. of ἐραννός, an adjective meaning 'lovely'.

οὐρανίην (sky) χθονίαν (earth) τε (both) καὶ (and) εἰναλίην (of the sea) - *in the sky, earth, as well as the sea*.

κροκόπεπλον - Ækáti is κροκόπεπλος (fem./masc. nom.), *adored with saffron-coloured robes*.

τυμβιδίην - *funereal*

ψυχαῖς (life or soul) νεκύων (corpse) μέτα (among) βακχεύουσαν (revel) - *Daimohn, celebrating among the corpses!*

Ækáti is associated with the Middle Sky, the area which extends from just above the sea and the land up to just below the moon. This is the place where the souls dwell, the souls of those whose mortal bodies have died and are awaiting rebirth. Ækáti likes to dwell in this region and assist the mortals and deities who reside there. The idea that the souls of the dead inhabit the lower sky can be found in various texts such as:

> 'All soul, whether without mind or with it, when it has issued from the body is destined to wander <in> the region between earth and moon...[72]

This idea can also be found in Pythagorean writings:

> 'When cast out upon the earth, it (ed. the soul) wanders in the air like the body. Hermes is the steward of souls, and for that reason is called Hermes the Escorter, Hermes the Keeper of the Gate, and Hermes of the Underworld, since it is he who brings in the souls from their bodies both by land and sea; and the pure are taken into the uppermost region, but the impure are not permitted to approach the pure or each other, but are bound by the Furies in bonds unbreakable.
> The whole air is full of souls which are called Genii or Heroes; these are they who send men dreams and signs of future disease and health, and not to men alone, but to sheep also and cattle as well; and it is to them that purifications and lustrations, all divination, omens and the like, have reference. The most momentous thing in human life is the art of winning the soul to good or to evil. Blest are the men who acquire a good soul; [if it be bad] they can never be at rest, nor ever keep the same course two days together.[73]

---

[72] (Πλούταρχος *Ἠθικά Concerning the Face Which Appears in the Orb of the Moon*, Chap. 28, 943C; trans. Harold Cherniss and William C. Helmbold, 1957, Public Domain).

[73] (Διογένης Λαέρτιος *The Lives and Opinions of Eminent Philosophers*, 8.31, trans. by C. D. Yonge, 1828.)

Περσείαν - *Persian*, because she is *the daughter of Pérsis* (Perses; Gr. Πέρσης).

φιλέρημον - *fond of solitude* (φιλέρημος, fem./masc. nom.).

ἀγαλλομένην (exult) ἐλάφοισι (deer) - *delighting in deer*.

νυκτερίην - Ækáti is called Νυκτέρια (fem. nom./voc. sing.), *nocturnal*, because her knowledge and activities are difficult to comprehend, as though hidden in the night. Her rituals were usually performed at night by torchlight. She is associated with the night sky, for her parents are stars, great sources of light which are only visible in the dark.

σκυλακῖτιν - Ækáti is σκυλακῖτις (nom., etym. from σκύλαξ, dog or whelp), *protectress of dogs*. Ártæmis (Artemis; Gr. Ἄρτεμις) uses 'dogs' to hunt down the beautiful souls; Ækáti uses the 'dogs' to deliver prayers to Gods. All people have an Agathós Daimohn (Gr. Ἀγαθὸς Δαίμων), a soul who accompanies you always and who loves and protects you; the Agathós Daimohn is thought of as like the faithful dog who follows its master everywhere and tries to protect him from danger.

ἀμαιμάκετον (irresistible) βασίλειαν (queen) - Ækáti is the *irresistible* or *indomitable queen* (ἀμαιμάκετος [masc./fem. nom.] βασίλεια [fem. nom.]).

ταυροπόλον - This epithet, ταυροπόλος (fem. nom.), has various meanings. It may mean *drawn in a carriage yoked by bulls* or it may mean *bull-herder*.

παντὸς (all) κόσμου (Kózmos) κληιδοῦχον (holding the keys) ἄνασσαν (queen) - *You are the queen who holds the keys to all the Kózmos*.

ἡγεμόνην - from ἡγεμονέω, *she who holds authority*.

νύμφην - *divine Nýmphi* (*girl* or *bride*; νύμφη is nom.).

κουροτρόφον - Ækáti is the κουροτρόφος (fem./masc. nom.), the *nurturer of children and youths*.

οὐρεσιφοῖτιν - Ækáti is οὐρεσιφοῖτις, *she who haunts the mountains*.

λισσόμενοις (pray) κούρην (maiden) τελεταῖς (rituals) ὁσίαισι (hallowed) παρεῖναι (let fall) - *Pray, Maiden, attend our hallowed rituals.*

βουκόλῳ (*βουκόλῳ*, herdsman) εὐμενέουσαν (graciousness) ἀεὶ (always) κεχαρηότι (rejoice, hail) θυμῷ (incense) - *Be always gracious to your herdsman (βούκολος* [no fem. form], a devotee of the Mysteries) *and rejoice in our gifts of incense.*

All this work yields a new translation of the hymn:

1. Ækáti (Εκάτη)
I call Ækáti of the Crossroads, worshipped at the meeting of three paths, oh lovely one.
In the sky, earth, and sea, you are venerated in your saffron-coloured robes.
Funereal Daimohn, celebrating among the souls of those who have passed.
Persian, fond of deserted places, you delight in deer.
Goddess of night, protectress of dogs, invincible Queen.
Drawn by a yoke of bulls, you are the Queen who holds the keys to all the Kózmos.
Commander, Nýmphi, nurturer of children, you who haunt the mountains.
Pray, Maiden, attend our hallowed rituals;
Be forever gracious to your mystic herdsman and rejoice in our gifts of incense.

The Importance of the Orphic Hymn in Modern Practice

Contributed by Christina Moraiti, Athens, Greece

Εἰνοδίην Ἑκάτην κλήιζω, τριοδῖτιν, ἐραννήν,
οὐρανίην, χθονίαν τε, καὶ εἰναλίην κροκόπεπλον,
τυμβιδίην, ψυχαῖς νεκύων μέτα βακχεύουσαν,
Πέρσειαν, φιλέρημον, ἀγαλλομένην ἐλάφοισιν,
νυκτερίην, σκυλακῖτιν, ἀμαιμάκετον βασίλειαν,
θηρόβρομον, ἄζωστον, ἀπρόσμαχον εἶδος ἔχουσαν,
ταυροπόλον, παντὸς κόσμου κληιδοῦχον ἄνασσαν,
ἡγεμόνην, νύμφην, κουροτρόφον, οὐρεσιφοῖτιν,
λισσόμενοις κούρην τελεταῖς ὁσίαισι παρεῖναι
βουκόλῳ εὐμενέουσαν ἀεὶ κεχαρηότι θυμῷ.

Hekate of the Roads, three-formed, lovely one, I call upon thee,
Of the sky, the earth and the sea, saffron-clad,
Funereal, you who rejoices among the souls of the dead,
Persis' only daughter, fond of solitude, the one who rejoices with deer,
Nocturnal, goddess of dogs, unconquerable Queen,
Heralded by wild beasts, free of belt, the one who cannot be defeated,
Bull mistress, Keybearer regent of the whole Cosmos,
Ruler, nymph, protector of children and mount wanderer,
Let us beg the Daughter for her benevolent presence,
in these sacred rituals,
Of the cow shepherd whose heart will rejoice.

The Orphic Hymn to the Goddess Hekate is recited on a daily basis by so many, but do we really understand the importance of it and its actual meaning? Word for word and beyond, what has been salvaged through the ages? Do we realise that every epithet attributed to the goddess Hekate, every word used in this hymn; derives from established worship of many hundreds of years? And what can we gain by the comprehension of this hymn today?

The Orphic Hymns in general have been subject to much research, speculation and inspiration for a very long time. Especially since modern polytheists, who feel the call of the Hellenic Gods, have as a reference a complete set of hymns that show both the attitude and the roles that each god or goddess possessed by the time of the hymn's creation. That creation is given between the 2nd and 3rd century CE in Asia Minor. That means that by then, the Roman Empire had an established rule over the Greek peninsula (that partly fell in 146 BCE after the battle of Corinth and was fully conquered by 27 BCE) and of course across the Aegean of Asia Minor alike. We need to remember that by the time of the creation of the hymns for each God and Goddess, their worship is known through the culture and lifestyle not only for the Athenians but all Greeks, since these three factors along with language are what was needed to form a common civilization (in more modern terms, a country or/and a nation).

What is also interesting, especially for the worshipers of the goddess Hekate, is that the Orphic Hymns are numbered and the hymn for the Lady of the Crossroads comes first, before any other deity. This is clearly due to Hekate's importance in Orphism and Neoplatonism and her salvaging role for souls and the afterlife. Both cases coincide with the creation of the hymns chronologically and link them. That automatically leads to the conclusion that for the hymn maker(s), Hekate plays a very important role in the way the cosmos works. It is not surprising given the location of the Hymns; Asia Minor was a place where the goddess Hekate was widely and magnificently worshipped in the city of Stratonikea and Lagina, with her temple being one of a kind in the Hellenistic and Roman period. We find her in a joint cult of the Great Mother Cybele as evidenced in the statues depicting the enthroned Queen and we also have traces of her worship in Didima, Ephesus and Aphrodisia. She was recognised in the greatest cities of Asia Minor and of course her depictions across the sea to the islands of Chalki, Rhodes, Kos and Samos are also of great importance. Her worship spreads from Northern Greece (Samothraki, Vergina, Pella, Amfipolis, Filipopolis etc) down to Thessaly (Melitea, Lamia, Larissa) to Athens and of course to Corinth and Epidaurus in the Peloponnese.

When we read a Hymn written as late as the 2nd century CE, we need to remember that they embraced a vast idea of how Hekate was worshipped, in what fields she was important, and how people perceived her. Worship evolved as much as society did and although the times of greatness from Classical Greece have long since passed, this hymn is proof of how diverse and expanded her role was in many different aspects of life. The context of her worship's magnitude at the time of the hymns' creation can explain the use of words adorning her with royalty and importance such as *'anassa', 'eranin', 'amaimaketon vasilian'* and *'igemonin'* all different ways to refer to her the attribute of Queen, no one with more significance than the other in the complicated Greek language. If someone who understands ancient Greek reads the Hymn to Hekate, they can notice that the epithets used are basically falling into three categories, one of *location* for her dominion, one of *personal attributes* to her and one showing her *importance* and the way she should be worshipped. Let us take each line to a small analysis so we can truly grasp their meaning while we keep in mind the context of the ancient times, of the language and therefore the people.

Since speaking of context: the Greek language did not have a formal way (honorific plural) of speaking to someone until the 19th century. The Greek-speaking world always valued logic and the practical, natural order of things. If they see one person (mortal or divine) they would speak directly in singular and only when they were before an audience or group did they use the arithmetic plural. So here, the Goddess is called upon directly like all other gods, which in itself creates an immediate communication, forming the culture of how people presented: loud and clear, standing and speaking straight to their Gods. All their respect, fear, love or complaint were poured through vocals and body language either when they spoke to respectful people or the rulers of the world aka the Gods.

Hekate of the Roads, three-formed, lovely one, I call upon thee

Here, Hekate is declared as the ruler of the roads, the one who looks in three directions since the crossroads were dangerous places for bandits, ambushes and wandering spirits that couldn't find their way to the afterlife. It was also a place where criminals were left unburied for everyone to see, always outside the protection of the city walls, the ultimate punishment of desecration in a time when the bodies of the deceased were so important that even Homer informs us of Achilles' awful treatment of Hector's body outside the walls of Troy. We can imagine a goddess with such heavy-duty should be at the least intimidating yet, here she's described as lovely and for an even more accurate translation of the ancient Greek word: loveable. This kind of loveliness is usually attributed to a Goddess young in age and pure in deeds. The Goddess shares many attributes with the Goddess Artemis, one of them being her image and epithets of the young woman, in many cases like in ancient Epidaurus where the great Temple of Artemis-Hekate stood in one of the most important places of worship. We find both Goddesses depicted as young and in short-hemmed dresses, practical for swift motion. We also have evidence from Brauron, Athens that young noble girls made sacrifices of animals to Artemis like in Stratonikeia the noble youth did to the goddess Hekate.

Of the sky (Ourania), the earth (Cthonia) and the sea (Einalia), saffron-clad

Hesiod informs us in his Theogony, approximately 900 years (730-700 BCE) before the Orphic Hymns, that Zeus preserves Hekate's rule over the Sky, the Earth and the Sea since she sided with him during the Titanomachy. That is verified here with the three epithets given to the Goddess. Ourania also means the one who lives in the sky (all Titans and gods were ouranoi). Ourania is also the epithet of Aphrodite when she is armed for her participation in divine battles against Titans and giants.

Chthonia is of the underworld but also the one who comes back and forth from the realm of the dead, stationed somewhere in between (wells, caves, rivers, hollows in the earth, cemeteries). This epithet also gives us the first sign that she is associated with both rites of death and rebirth, like the Eleusinian and Samothracian mysteries, but also practices of witchcraft (goetia) practices, for which the Chthonian gods were pivotal.

Last but not least, Einalia takes care of the sea and everything upon and in it, a very important epithet for sea people like the Greeks and the tumultuous tides of the Aegean. The epithet Krokopeplon (saffron clad) shows her magnificence as saffron was always expensive and rare to find, used in fabrics for royalty since the times as back as of Ancient Thera (Santorini). Her connection to Hermes can also be shown with this epithet as Krokos (or saffron) was a young athlete whom Hermes killed by accident and transformed the youth into this rare and beautiful flower.

Funereal, you who rejoices among the souls of the dead

The one involved in funerals and everything that has to do with them. Entire books have been written for ancient funeral rites in ancient Greece, of the culture around the dead, the demons and how people dealt with the inevitable. What is more important about them is for us to know the context: when someone was about to die, the Greeks believed that specific gods were upon them to receive the soul; for the soul was very important and something to fear, if it didn't find peace. It could become a tool for magicians to send towards people, it could haunt the living. Death was a very common occurrence, but people feared it all the same, and the dead who couldn't find peace at the time of death were a very literal problem for the Greeks. That meant that offerings to the Gods who either pacified or commanded the dead had to be made first, satisfied and merciful with their duty; they were very important and quite frequent in their service. Here we also see the Goddess as the one who rejoices with the souls of the dead, leading us to understand that her duty - although a heavy and macabre one - was taken upon herself gladly. A goddess accustomed to the life cycles and the way death naturally reached the elderly and untimely even the unborn, she was always there to take care of them all.

Persis' only daughter, fond of solitude, the one who rejoices with deer

Usually, the epithets of origin with the name of the father are called for only children, especially only daughters and virgins since there is no master of them (aka husband). In this case, we see both the importance of the origin (the great Titan of destruction) and the magnificence of how old her presence in the world really is, as she's a Titaness who ruled the world when the original six children of Rhea and Cronus hadn't even been conceived yet. She's friendly to solitude, as not many women had the privilege to be, and she is rejoicing with deer. These two epithets give us the idea of her ruling over places where not many people go (cemeteries, the cities at night, forests and lonely paths) and of course places of nature where there must be peace for the easily frightened deer to exist, let alone live freely. The deer in many cultures is seen as the symbol of freedom, innocence, pureness and speed. Of course here we also see her connection with her cousin again, the Goddess Artemis.

Nocturnal, Goddess of dogs, unconquerable Queen

The one of the night, where spirits exist and shadows are lost to darkness, is everywhere. Yet she is also there casting shadows anew, as she lights the way with her torches. Quite a few festivals took place at night, and most frequent were the Oxithimia that were in honour of the goddess Hekate. After cleaning their homes of everything impure and vile, people put the *katharmoi*, the impurities, in clay vessels and left them at crossroads, close to Hekate's statues without looking back, for the Goddess to take care and dispose of the negative energies.

The Goddess of dogs, her sacred animal from the legend of Hekabe, the woman of Troy who in her madness from losing both husband and son in the war with the Greeks cursed the Gods. Committing hubris, she flung herself from the walls of Troy, only for the goddess Hekate (in some cases, Artemis) to take pity on her and transform her into a howling black hound, sacred to the goddess Hekate, who accompanies her in the night. It is known that puppies were sacrificed to Hekate and were taken from house to house in cathartic rites. Nikandros (3rd century BCE) informs us that large black dogs from ancient Epirus were made by the God Hephaestus and they are called *Molossoi*. Myth has it that these dogs come as breeds sired by Cerberus, succeeded by Molossos the grandson of Achilles, and therefore became Hekate's guarding dogs.

The unconquerable Queen, in battle as this specific epithet reveals, demonstrates the epic proportions that have been used since the Homeric tales to describe her. Here, she is unmatched in battle with her title as a ruler, again verifying her importance in the realms she presides over. The epithet is also explained as the 'furious Queen'.

Heralded by wild beasts, free of belt, the one who cannot be defeated

Beasts signalled Hekate's arrival. We know this from the legends of how Hekate saved the city of Byzantium, by causing the dogs of the city to scream and alert the people before the attack of the Macedonians. Goddesses of nature often have this attribute, as they coax a reaction by animals and their arrival always stirs a response. Free of the belt, the swift one, the quick and unstoppable; the lack of belt and its mention shows a Goddess who is fast and always on the move, one who travels frequently, and is not easily still. The one who simply cannot lose in battle, another powerful epithet showing her agility and stamina, an epithet worthy of a warrior.

Bull mistress, Keybearer regent of the whole Cosmos

Protector of the bulls, and one closely associated with this specific animal. Like Artemis, Hekate is *Tavropolos* and the bull played a massive role in the culture of the Greeks since Minoan Crete, where men leapt over the massive animal in a rite of passage that gave them a seat among the world of grown men. We have depictions from places such as Samothrace, Lagina, Eleusis and Thessaly, where the bull was associated with sites of worship of the goddess Hekate. The bull is also a sacrificial animal that symbolises both strength and purity; we even have Zeus himself transforming into a bull so he can approach Europa and also Demeter; from the union with the latter, Persephone was born.

The keybearer Queen of the whole world, again epic epithets showing the Goddess' importance. Keybearers were always part of the priesthood and played important roles in the functioning of the temples on a regular basis, but also during important festivals for the Gods each temple belonged to. Here we can see a universal role for Hekate, probably associated with her World Soul aspect, where she opens and closes the gates between the realms. Chronologically connecting Orphism, Neoplatonism, the hymn and the Chaldean Oracles of which we have only fragments today.

Ruler, nymph, protector of children and mount wanderer

This epithet also shows us her sovereignty and also the epithet of *Nymph*, proving her youth and virginal aspect as only young girls and very young women were regarded as nymphs. In many cases, noble girls who served as priestesses of Artemis dressed as Nymphs during festivals for the Goddess of the Hunt. We must also note that girls stopped serving the Goddess once they hit puberty and in general, women couldn't stay maidens forever since social norms would have them married off - or at best, dedicated to a husband at a fairly young age. Or they would be promised as virgins to serve Goddesses for their entire lives with grave punishments if that virginity was lost.

The importance of the virginity in goddesses like Hekate, Athena, Artemis and Hestia and the implications of Persephone's abduction, is in contrast with what people understand of the Victorian translation of the myth. Hades didn't rape Persephone, he wouldn't stand the violation as Hera would never bless the King of the Underworld for his union with the future Queen. The symbolism of death, sudden or expected; no matter how hard we try to deal with it; would be lost. Hades *snatched* her (something that was rare but not unheard of in the Greek-speaking world at least until the 19th century, in many cases with the validity of the woman involved) and in his effort to keep her lawfully in the Underworld, he married her and offered her the pomegranate.

But let's go back to Hekate and her epithet of *Kourotrophos*, the one who takes care of children and animals, again shared with Artemis. We know this epithet is given to her in places of worship like Epidaurus and Brauron and we see her standing silently at the side of reliefs while a labour is taking place, ready to take care of the child, dead or alive, in a time when childbirth was very dangerous. We know she's taking care of the little ones, she is present in Athenian houses, in the deepest part of the *'oikos'* and we have evidence of young children bearing the key during the festival at Stratonikea.

A mount wanderer who is one with nature and thrives in caves and mountains. We know people built temples in hard to reach spots at the top of mountains and cliffs, wishing to be as high and close to the sky as possible. It's no coincidence that the Greeks believed their Gods resided upon the highest mount of Greece, Mount Olympus. We can see she's an enduring Goddess who is allowed to travel between the realms; in this case, from the sky down to the earth and as we have already seen, even deeper still.

<u>*Let us beg the Daughter for her benevolent*</u>
<u>*presence in these sacred rituals*</u>
<u>*Of the cow shepherd whose heart will rejoice*</u>

This is the conclusion of the hymn and the part that is most interesting, in my opinion, as here we see a clear declaration towards a young, benevolent Goddess who is asked to be present in rites in her name. The calling comes from the bull shepherds and this points to rural worship, although we have evidence of the goddess Hekate being present within cities and even at the hearts of them, such as the ancient Agora of Athens and even upon the Acropolis as Epipiridia, guarding the entrance of the temples that lead to the Parthenon. It's very interesting how here we have this specific mention of bull shepherds as the *'voukolos'* the one who has herds of bulls, and although we're not sure why the shepherds would be mentioned in such an epic declaration of the Goddess' roles and attributes, it is clear that she was present in the circles of nature, human and animal life and of course death.

This is the hymn and a small analysis of it, we understand from the way it is made and the priority it gets as the first hymn, that whoever wrote it kept the goddess Hekate in high regard. But it has always baffled me why people in ancient times created hymns in the first place, loud and robust while the new religions created prayers, plunged in silence or privacy. The answer to the question came to me when I realised the fundamental difference between *'piste'* faith/belief and *'latreia'* adoration/worship of the divine. On one hand, the best-case scenario is for a sighting of God or the Holy Mother in signs, dreams, visions or at best in real life momentarily. In the other, the Gods reveal themselves and *interact* with humans, they demand things, fall in love with them, help them in their quests actively and even transform them into demi-gods or sacred animals and heroes either in their mercy or condemnation. This incredible difference between the faith in something distant and the adoration of something so intimate and immediate changes the mentality of the people.

Of course, if you fall in love and adore or worship beings as magnificent as a god or goddess, you may both love and fear them. There are examples in the myths of where this leads to envy and theft, and even severe punishment. You may find yourself calling out the hymns to the gods, in the knowledge that it does not mask their failures and that they also get mad, commit crimes and misdeeds.

Their stories are not ones of torture and martyrdom but of passion, revenge, love, hatred, hope, jealousy, protection and competition. That makes them eternally loved, familiar and understood by mortals. No god or goddess truly dies; even if killed, their absolute power will always bring them back as something new, better, a greater version of what they were before.

Faith is illogical, a Christian priest once told me, in answer to my question about the belief in a God who is benevolent but who drowned humanity with only Noah and his kin surviving. A God who killed the firstborns of the Egyptians, a God who gives children cancer today. I refused to accept this answer, 'Eternal happiness in the Kingdom of Heaven' seemed like a lie in a game with a rigged dice. Then, I turned towards the ways of my ancestors, which, until then, I had only learned about in fairytales and myths, stories of 'the poor ancient people' who didn't know any better than to create the Gods in this way. The same ancient people whose culture had been known as the pillar of western ideas and our way of life. The creators of maths, democracy, theatre, poetry, politics, philosophy, astronomy and strategy among others; they seemed to have been great, but in the matters of their religion... at least according to the Christians who followed the destruction of the ancient world and survived to control the narrative.

Faith bypasses logic, and takes the agency of the one demanding the answer to the unfair and the injustice. "Only God knows," was the most common answer for the starving children of Africa, the poor and the dying of AIDS and cancer without painkillers, the rich with all the amenities. But Worship is something different, derived from the mind. The ancient Greeks were practical people who valued the *'nous'*, the mind, they regarded natural and physical beauty but above all, they valued logic. These same people were not 'blessed' by their gods but they were *'evnooumenoi'*, favoured by the Gods, with the insight of the mind and the logic of the Gods themselves.

Worship changes the mindset, it answers the questions easily because the context and the paradox of the all-mighty and good God is gone. Gods have passions like us, the order of things gives great misfortunes to all, divine or not, the human race finds solace in and identifies with the misfortunes of the Gods themselves. Demeter mourns the loss of her precious daughter, Hera is jealous of Zeus, Zeus gets furious, Aphrodite commits adultery, Ares is a coward, Hephestus has a disability, Athena gets angry with humans like Arachne, Hekate can torture people with her demons, Poseidon is vengeful of Odysseus and so on, the examples are so many.

DOES THAT MEAN THE GODS ARE EVIL?

No, the gods are magnificent, they are amazing, and they protect humans. For Demeter teaches us agriculture, Hera protects women and marriage. Zeus is the father of all, just and protector of the 'xenoi', the foreigners. Aphrodite protects people in love and even Ares gives a way for his appeasement and sets rules in war. Hephestus is one of the most caring to the humans and Athena protects Athens, favours Prometheus and Odysseus in their adventures among others, whilst Hekate protects athletes and kings and Poseidon keeps the earth from moving, preventing the destruction of earthquakes.

That difference, the view of the gods both as furious beings and also benevolent figures is what makes them so fascinating, it's the reason why we feel so familiar to them, so close that we end up worshipping and/or adoring exactly those values and aspects, requesting of them directly to help us or to be furious toward our own enemies. It's precisely the reason they are also fascinated with us, so much that we have stories of gods and goddesses persuading and seducing mortal men and women, even being rejected by us or helping when hopeless love stories unfold before them, for they become emotional for our suffering. We have age old stories of how the ephemeral and the eternal united and created heroes, kings, monsters and mythical creatures that served either as curses or gifts upon the world. So worship is based on logic, because the context is clear, there is no good god or evil god, there is only good and evil in all of us, mortals or not. There is no one to blame and no one to fear but our own limits and morals and deeds, just like the gods. No devil will burn us in eternal hell; for the guilt sent by the gods in our mind will drive us to fix our faults or simply lose that mind because of our injustice. By living a life in an ethical and harmless way, people were most likely to enjoy Elysium after death, a place where the sun always shone. If not, Tartarus would keep us away in a place of mental torture and if the judges of the underworld couldn't decide, the human would remain in the Asphodel Fields, where the mind would forget everything from the life it led and people would also forsake the deceased, a fortune worse than torture, many would say. We are favoured by the gods, when some misfortune befalls us, we can ask for help and guidance and we can cleanse ourselves and our space. If we think like the Greeks, we would believe that some demon was sent by another human upon us, or perhaps we had angered some god or goddess. Even if the answer seems scary, it is an answer that can help us improve instead of staying in the unknown of a distant god, sending illness or taking away our child to test us.

We can distinguish faith from worship even in the iconography of the different religions. The Christians beheaded the ancient statues or carved crosses in the eyes of the gods depicted in marble for a reason. They knew that in worship, the statue itself was ensouled by the priesthood. The eyes were the linking point with the humans who looked up to it for they needed answers in their prayers. Therefore, when the hymn was recited, you would be standing before the oversized adorned statue of the god or goddess, causing yourself to look *up* where the incense was blowing in the temple and even out of it to the skies and each word would be carried with it to the god or goddess who was called upon and inside that very statue. An immediate and intimate worship of a magnificent being reaching humans from above or below, depending on the festival and rite. Nothing compared to the distance and barrier created by the flat surface of an icon or even a non-adorned statue that rarely looks towards the believer or the absence of the animation of god altogether. In most cases, the objects of faith are at eye-level or texts are given to people to read from inside, keeping the head lowered, hands clasped before the body instead of opened towards the divine, inward, while the ritual is taking place in most cases in versions of the language that the believer doesn't even properly understand.

These differences make the ancient hymns important today, in a period where the tides are changing once again, giving us freedom and agency in our lives and our personal paths. We need to understand the vast contrast between the ways of following an Abrahamic religion (that many of us immersed ourselves involuntarily as children) and the different context of how we could and should worship our chosen gods, after realising the distinctive ways they work within the Cosmos and how our ancestors preserved these ideas and ways of the world.

Hekate in the Living Orphic Tradition

Contributed by Ariadne Rainbird, South Wales Valley, UK

First, a little background about me, how I discovered this path and what I mean by the Living Orphic Tradition. As a small child, the Greek myths were my bedtime reading. I was fascinated by tales of gods and heroes, how the natural world was inhabited by nymphs and daemons, and by how closely entwined the realms of gods and mortals were. Also, the wisdom and lessons about life, the importance of virtue and the heroic quest, of piety and honour, the dangers of Hubris (pride) and other moral lessons, the myths contain.

My love of the Greek Gods was further inspired through school and college days through their appearance in English literature, from Chaucer to Shakespeare and the English poets. At University, I was introduced to Plato for the first time, as well as Classical Greek plays. I also became involved in Buddhism and Yoga, and then in the Fellowship of Isis, and began exploring various pagan traditions. Upon moving to Wales, I was initiated into a Wiccan coven, with Wicca being my main path for several years. Living in Wales, I also learned about the Welsh Celtic tradition, as well as studying Heathenry for a year or so. But the Greek Gods continued to call to me, and I wanted to honour them not just as part of an eclectic Wiccan or neo-pagan tradition, but by exploring more traditionally Greek ways. I initially became involved in some online Hellenic pagan communities - had some good, some bad, some ugly and some crazy experiences - but eventually, in my search, I discovered (one version of) the living Orphic tradition.

We are lucky that much has survived in terms of written and material evidence of Ancient Greek paganism, which gives those who wish to practise Reconstructionist Greek Religion a wealth of information from which to piece together the ancient religions. Although much has been lost, far too much has also survived for the religion to ever have been destroyed completely. What's more, the philosophies continued to be developed in the works of the Platonist philosophers over the following centuries up to the present day.

There are still families in Greece who have practised pagan traditions that have been passed down and practised through generations, developing organically and naturally through the centuries, though firmly rooted in the myths, philosophies and spiritual practices of the ancient mystery traditions. Each family has its own traditions, and each is slightly or sometimes greatly different from the other. I have learned something of one of the family traditions from Greeks who are willing to share their tradition. This is very different to Hellenic Reconstructionism, which attempts to recreate mainstream rituals of Ancient and Classical Greece, but is a tradition that includes ideas and practices that have developed through the philosophical schools throughout the centuries but based in the mystical traditions known as Orphic. The Orphic philosophical tradition is often very different to mainstream practices and beliefs, and the Theoi (the gods) in particular may be interpreted very differently. Most pagans and goddess worshippers are aware of Hekate's role as Mistress of magic and goddess of witchcraft, but in the Orphic tradition, Hekate's role is a bit different. She is a goddess who embodies virtue and the mystic path, she is a savioress (*Soteira*) and mediator. She is considered to be the advocate of the virtuous. She is also seen as the World Soul, as described in the Chaldean Oracles and by the later Platonic philosophers.

First a bit about Orphism, as understood in the Living Tradition. Orphismos (or Orphism) is a mystery tradition or group of traditions, within Hellenismos (or Hellenism), closely connected with the Bacchic mysteries, and is often known as the Bacchic-Orphic mysteries. It can be seen as the religion of Dionysos, who in Orphismos is *Soter*, the Saviour. It is also closely connected with the Eleusinian mysteries, with Persephone also having an important role as *Soteira*, Saviouress. The Gold Tablets, often referred to as the Bacchic-Orphic Tablets, were discovered in burials of Bacchic-Orphic initiates throughout ancient Greece and Rome dating from the 5th century BCE to the 3rd Century CE. They contain funerary inscriptions giving instructions for the afterlife, in which Persephone and Dionysos are petitioned, or where the initiate is instructed to tell Persephone that they have been liberated by Dionysos himself. For example, a late 4th century BCE tablet from a woman's grave in Pelinna, Thessaly says:

> *Now you have died and now you have come into being.*
> *O thrice happy one, on this same day.*
> *Tell Persephone that the Bacchic One himself has released you...*
> *As a bull you jumped into the milk,*
> *Quickly you jumped into the milk...*
> *You have wine as your fortunate honour*
> *And below the earth there are ready for you the same prizes as for the blessed ones.*

And from another 4th Century BCE grave of a woman:

> *I come from the pure, Queen of the Chthonian Ones*
> *Eucles and Euboleus*[74] *and the gods and other daimones*
> *For I also claim to be of your happy race.*
> *I have paid for the penalty of unrighteous deeds.*
> *Either Moira overcame me or the star-flinger of lightnings.*
> *Now I come as a suppliant to holy Persephone,*
> *So that she may kindly send me to the seats of the pure.*

---

[74] Eucles (Good Fame) and Euboleus (Good Counsel) are epithets of Dionysos, Euboleus is associated with the Eleusinian mysteries as a torchbearer, leading initiates back from the darkness of the Underworld.

And a rather interesting (but fragmentary and interspersed with untranslatable letters, possibly magical formulas) one from Italy, full of specifically Orphic references:

> *To Protogonos, Earth Mother, Cybele, Daughter of Demeter,*
> *Zeus, Air, Sun, Fire that overcomes, Fortune,*
> *Phanes, All-remembering Moirai, Father, Master of All*
> *correspondence, Air, Fire, Mother, Night, Day. Seventh*
> *Day of a Fast, Zeus who digs in, and Watcher over all,*
> *always, Mother hear my prayers, beautiful sacred things,*
> *sacred things, Demeter, Fire, Zeus, Cthonic Kore. Hero,*
> *light to the mind, the mindful one seizes Kore. Land, Air, to*
> *the mind.*

And from the same area from a small tumulus:

> *I come from the pure, Queen of the Cthonian Ones*
> *Eucles, Euboleus and the other immortal Gods*
> *For I also claim to be of your happy race.*
> *But Moira overcame me and the other immortal Gods and*
> *the star-flinger with lightning.*
> *I have flown out of the heavy, difficult circle,*
> *I have approached the longed-for crown with swift feet,*
> *I have sunk beneath the breast of the Lady, the Cthonian*
> *Queen,*
> *I have approached the longed-for crown with swift feet,*
> *"happy and blessed, you will be a god instead of a mortal".*
> *As a kid I fell into the milk.*

Being a goat-kid leaping into the milk is a common feature of the Orphic tablets, and its mystical interpretation, at least in the tradition as I have learned it, is that the milk is the breast milk of Hera, Queen of the Gods, which is the milky way and that the liberated soul is leaping out into the Kosmos, as a goat-kid or a bull (animals associated with Dionysos) having flown out of 'the heavy, difficult circle' of rebirth, being nourished by the wine-aethir of Dionysos and deified, they are going forth as a god instead of a mortal, having achieved liberation and deification of the soul, which is the desired culmination of the Orphic path.

So, you may ask, what has all this got to do with Hekate? She is not mentioned in any of these Orphic tablets, so how in Orphism is Hekate Soteira, Saviouress? Why do we need her, when we have Persephone and Dionysos as Soteira/Soter? Well, Hekate does have an important place in Orphismos, as it is significant that Her hymn appears at the beginning of the Orphic Hymns, immediately after the instruction to Mouseus. In the Orphic Hymn to Hekate, she is described as holding the keys to the whole Kosmos, and being venerated in earth, sea and sky, as well as in the realm of the dead. She is therefore a goddess who can traverse the realms, a psychopomp, walker between the worlds and guide of souls, much like Hermes. Hekate is also found in the Orphic Argonautica - Orpheus invokes her in order to gain entry into the grove which harbours the Krysómallon Dǽras - the Golden Fleece. In Orphic interpretation, the Golden Fleece symbolises the deified soul, and therefore, Hekate is opening the gateway to the deification of the soul.

Hekate also had an important role in the Eleusinian mysteries and was one of the chief goddesses honoured in them, alongside Demeter and Persephone. In the story of the abduction of Persephone and Demeter's search for her daughter, Hekate was the one goddess who aided Demeter, as she had heard the cries of Persephone as she was abducted by Ploutohn and helped her in the search for her daughter, bearing torches to guide her. Hekate also became the chief handmaiden of Persephone in Hades. As assistant to Demeter and handmaid to Persephone, this subsidiary role might seem like a bit of a demotion to those who worship Hekate as the great goddess, Queen of the earth, sea and sky, holder of the keys to the Kosmos etc. But in fact, in Orphismos, Hekate's role as mediator is extremely important, and we need to understand what is meant by her role as mediator and advocate of the virtuous. As the goddess who is the mediator between (in Neo Platonic terms) the intelligible and sensible realms, between the realm of divine forms and that of the physical world, who facilitates passage from one realm to the other, It is Hekate who facilitates Persphone's journey. Homer tells us in the Homeric Hymn to Demeter, that *'Queen Hekate was the predecessor and the follower of Persephone'*, which conjures an image of Hekate as surrounding and protecting Persephone. Hekate is present at Persephone's descent, and her return, and as her guide, companion and handmaiden, escorting Persephone on a very difficult and significant journey and continues to escort Her across the boundary and ease her transition in her annual descent and ascent. As mistress of souls, Hekate also escorts the dead back and forth across this same boundary.

It might be helpful at this stage to say a little about the basic principles of the living Orphic tradition as I have learned it, in order to give a context for understanding the importance of Hekate's role as mediator and advocate of the virtuous. I have already mentioned the importance of Dionysos, Soter, the saviour, and Persephone Soteira, the saviouress in the tradition. Orphic myth says (at least in the version most commonly cited in this tradition), that Zeus seduced Persephone in the form of a serpent, and she subsequently gave birth to Zagreus (the first birth of Dionysos, known as Zeus's first influence on the soul), whom Zeus intended to be his successor as king of the Gods. Zeus gave the infant Zagreus his staff, thunderbolts and throne. However, at the instruction of Hera, the Titans distracted the infant Zagreus with a number of toys (each of which has mystical significance).

> *'A pine cone and a spinning top, and limb-moving rattles, and golden apples from the clear-toned Hesperides, where apples grew which bestowed mortality, dice, a sphere, a top, tufts of fleece and a mirror. Zagreus was delighted with the toys, and abandoned his thunderbolts, and whilst He contemplated His changeling countenance reflected in the mirror, Mesmerised, beholding of himself, he proceeded into the whole fabrication of the universe. The Titans took that opportunity to seize him, and destroyed him with infernal*

> *knives. Seven parts of the child in all did they divide between them.'*

The toys of Dionysos all have mystical or magical significance – and the spinning top particularly is associated with Hekate (the Iynx-wheel), which is used to mediate between the realms and is associated with Iynges, or Daemons which mediate between the Divine and mortal realms, and which are under the dominion of Hekate.

When Zeus got to hear of this, he destroyed the Titans with thunderbolts - but the heart of Zagreus was saved and placed in a silver casket and taken by Athena to a place of safety. Zeus then created the races of mortals from the ashes of the Titans and the burned remains of the limbs of Zagreus. Thus, the mortal races are created from the sinful substance of the Titans, which binds them to the cycle of death and rebirth; and the divinity of Dionysos Zagreus, through whom liberation may be achieved.

Zeus then made a potion from the heart of Zagreus which he gave to Semele, semi-divine daughter of the Goddess Harmonia and the mortal King Cadmus to drink. Semele then became pregnant with the infant Dionysos, and the birth of Dionysos on earth through Semele is known as Zeus's second influence on the soul. Dionysos is sent as a saviour and liberator to aid us to escape from the cycles of rebirth and to achieve gnosis of our divinity and reunion with the Divine. Persephone has an important role both as the first mother of Dionysos, and as a compassionate receiver of souls who births us into the next life. Her role in mythology of continually descending and ascending, represents the soul incarnating back into matter, and being liberated and reunited with the Divine.

Along with Dionysos, who may be seen as the central figure of Orphismos, the 12 Olympians are also honoured, each one having an important role in guiding the human soul on the path to liberation, and each also connected with a sign of the Zodiac, the wheel around the central hub that Dionysos represents.

The Orphic path itself can be said to have Four Pillars. The first is Akoi, 'things heard', which relates to the traditions, stories of the gods, the myths, rituals, practices and philosophies. The second is Theurgy - divine work - which in the tradition is seen as communion with deity through ritual and meditative practices. The third is Philosophia, which is the love of and striving for wisdom, and refers to intellectual work which endeavours to discover genuine truth and wisdom and to challenge our own ideas, the raw philosophy of Sokrates, rather than self-justifying philosophical theories. So, on the one hand, there is the tradition, what we are taught, and on the other there is our questioning of all beliefs and the scrutiny of everything with the rational eye of philosophy. The fourth pillar is perhaps the most important, and that is Areti, which may be translated as virtue or excellence. This is not the pursuit of glory as some understand the word due to the way it is used in ancient texts such as Homer's Iliad, but is the source from which all virtues are generated. Plato said that Areti is a kind of harmony of the soul, a type of constant between one's emotions and one's reason. Plato also described four principle manifestations of Areti: Courage or fortitude, Temperance or Moderation, Wisdom, and Justice. These are the four Cardinal Virtues of Classical Antiquity. The development of Areti involves understanding one's place in the Kosmos and living in accordance with the Natural Laws, whilst seeking to develop one's Consciousness, and to be the best that one can be. In the living Orphic tradition, the striving for and achievement of Areti is the most pleasing gift we can offer to the gods. The gods desire us to achieve Areti and endeavour to help us to achieve it, if we put the effort in.

Hekate, She who has Far-Shooting Power, is the mighty goddess who is our greatest advocate in the pursuit of *areti* (arete; Gr. ἀρετή), genuine virtue.

Hekate first appears in Greek literature in Hesiod, in Works and Days, which tells us:

'And Astæria conceived by Perses, and bare Hekate whom Zeus the son of Kronos honoured above all. He gave her splendid gifts, to have a share of the earth and the unfruitful sea. She received honour also in starry heaven, and is honoured exceedingly by the deathless Gods. For to this day, whenever any one of men on earth offers rich sacrifices and prays for favour according to custom, he calls upon Hekate. Great honour comes full easily to him whose prayers the Goddess receives favourably, and she bestows wealth upon him; for the power surely is with Her. For as many as were born of Gaia and Ouranos amongst all these She has her due portion. The son of Kronos did her no wrong nor took anything away of all that was Her portion among the former Titan Gods: but she holds, as the division was at the first from the beginning, privilege both in earth, and in heaven, and in sea. Also, because She is an only child, the Goddess receives not less honour, but much more still, for Zeus honours her. Whom She will, She greatly aids and advances: She sits by worshipful kings in judgement, and in the assembly whom She will is distinguished among the people. And when men arm themselves for the battle that destroys men, then the Goddess is at hand to give victory and grant glory readily to whom She will. Good is She also when men contend at the games, for there too the Goddess is with them and profits them: and he who by might and strength gets the victory wins the rich prize easily with joy, and brings glory to his parents. And She is good to stand by horsemen, whom She will: and to those whose business is in the grey discomfortable sea, and who pray to Hekate and the loud-crashing Earth-Shaker, easily the glorious Goddess gives great catch, and easily she takes it away as soon as seen, if so She will. She is good in the byre with Hermes to increase the stock. The droves of kine and wide herds of goats and flocks of fleecy sheep, if She will, She increases from a few, or makes many to be less. So, then, albeit Her mother's only child, She is honoured amongst all the deathless Gods. And the son of Kronos made her a nurse of the young who after that day saw with their eyes the light of all-seeing Dawn. So from the beginning She is a nurse of the young, and these are her honours.'

This passage in Hesiod has sometimes been considered to be an Orphic intrusion into Works and Days, as it seems to appear out of nowhere, and does not follow the context of the rest of the work. Hekate was thought in Hesiod's time to be a minor deity, yet Hesiod suddenly goes into a quite lengthy hymn of praise and exultation to Hekate, which appears to mark her out as a very important deity. Yet following this passage, Hekate plays no further role in the Theogony. This Hymn to Hekate appears just before the account of the birth of Zeus and the other Olympians. Hekate is the last-born of the older Gods (with the exception of the sons of Iapetus). The Theogony concludes with the triumph of Zeus and the Olympian order, and the story of Prometheus and the creation of man and woman. The Olympians rule supreme, with Zeus at their head, yet we are told in the passage about Hekate that *'Zeus honoured Hekate above all and gave Her splendid gifts, to have a share of earth and the sterile sea. And She also received a share of honour from the starry sky'.* Here, the Greek is quite precise in saying that Hekate is not given earth, sea and sky, but that She is given (or rather retains) a *share* of honour on earth, heavens and sea. The notion of a portion or share is repeated throughout the Hymn. During the battle with the Titans, Zeus promised all who aided Him on his side, that they would be allowed to keep the honour they held previously, and whoever had been without honour or privilege under Cronos would receive both. Hekate does not appear to have a role in the Titanomachy, or to render any special services to Zeus, yet She not only keeps her honours but receives new ones. The text stresses that it is Zeus who honours Her, not the other way round, as if Zeus himself sees the importance of keeping in Hekate's favour and maintaining Her functions in His new regime. Hekate is called *Mounogenes* 'only daughter', indicating Her unique position over the three Cosmic Realms. Hekate's powers over the lives of men are also listed, and it is clear that Hekate's good will assures the success of every human endeavour, but it is also clear, that this is given in conjunction with other deities, as can be seen from this passage:

> "...*to those whose business is in the grey discomfortable sea, and who pray to Hekate and the loud-crashing Earth-Shaker, easily the glorious Goddess gives great catch, and easily she takes it away as soon as seen, if so She will. She is good in the byre with Hermes to increase the stock. The droves of kine and wide herds of goats and flocks of fleecy sheep, if She will, She increases from a few, or makes many to be less...*"

In this passage, prayers to Hekate work in conjunction with prayers to Poseidon in the first instance, and to Hermes in the second instance. Similarly, she grants pre-eminence in war, and brings victory and glory, yet this is the realm of Nike, who dwells with Zeus and with Athena. Hekate therefore has extensive, but not fully independent powers. She has an influence in each realm, but manifests her powers in areas which belong to other gods or to a diversity of gods. But, in each sphere, it is the good will of Hekate that ensures success. If Hekate's good will is absent, the implication is that prayers and offerings will be useless and failure will follow.

In the Living Orphic Tradition, Hekate is called the Advocate of the Virtuous, because it is by cultivating Areti, or Virtue, that one can win the favour of the goddess who has the power over success or failure in all realms.

So, Ækáti is the mighty advocate of the virtuous who holds our hands while we pray, allowing the Agathós <u>Daimohn</u>, (Gr. Ἀγαθὸς Δαίμων), represented by her dogs, to take our prayers to the gods. The agathas daimones can take our supplications to be heard by the Olympian Gods. Hekate will always listen to those who strive for virtue, and her dogs will take our prayers to the Olympians, advocating on our behalf.

When a person decides to commit to a life of virtue, the gods take notice, as though their eyes open wide; and they move close to us and give help, for they know that this is a difficult road, and they find such an endeavour beautiful. Ækáti is particularly interested in the souls of those who embark on this pursuit. She assists the suppliant and works alongside Athiná (Athena; Gr. Ἀθηνᾶ) who, according to the Orphic Rhapsodic Theogony is virtue itself.

Ækáti is the Queen of Mayeia, Ækáti is the great Goddess of Mayeia (mageia; Gr. μᾰγεία). She has intimate knowledge of and control of the natural world and is capable of using this power to great ability in order to assist worthy mortals. This mayeia, or magic, does not defy natural laws but is, by its very nature, only available to evolved beings who are in harmony with the natural laws such that they reflect its power and can employ it, souls such as the genuine Iærophántis (Hierophant; Gr. Ἱεροφάντης) at the Ælefsínia Mystíria and Gods. Such mayeia is exercised for the benefit of the virtuous when in need.

Ækáti is often considered a 'dark' goddess and is often connected with witchcraft and magic. Ækáti is called *Nyktǽria* (Gr. Νυκτέρια), an epithet meaning 'of the night'. This is because, like the Goddess Nyx, Ækáti operates in areas that are generally unknown to mortals and inaccessible to the rational mind, hence they are hidden from us as though concealed by night. But Ækáti is the daughter of Astæría, the starry one, and Pǽrsis, who is also connected with the stars and fire; therefore, even though her parents are connected with the night, they are of the stars, celestial bodies which give light, but which can only be perceived in darkness. One of Ækáti's epithets is *phohsphóros* (phosphorus; Gr. φωσφόρος), an epithet meaning 'bringing light.' Ækáti has hidden means to give help, but particularly when we cannot see our way through difficult problems.

Ækáti is associated with the Middle Sky, the area which extends from just above the sea and the land up to just below the moon. This is the place where the souls dwell, the souls of those whose mortal bodies have died and are awaiting rebirth. As such, she is dwelling with the dead. Although Hekate has a portion of earth, sea and sky, she likes to dwell in this middle region and assist the mortals and deities who reside there. The idea that the souls of the dead inhabit the middle sky can be found in various texts such as Plutarch:

> *'All soul, whether without mind or with it, when it has issued from the body is destined to wander in the region between earth and moon...'*[75]

This idea can also be found in Pythagorean writings:

> *'When cast out upon the earth, the soul wanders in the air like the body. Hermes is the steward of souls, and for that reason is called Hermes the Escorter, Hermes the Keeper of the Gate, and Hermes of the Underworld, since it is he who brings in the souls from their bodies both by land and sea; and the pure are taken into the uppermost region, but the impure are not permitted to approach the pure or each other, but are bound by the Furies in bonds unbreakable. The whole air is full of souls which are called Genii or Heroes; these are they who send men dreams and signs of future disease and health, and not to men alone, but to sheep also and cattle as well; and it is to them that purifications and lustrations, all divination, omens and the like, have reference. The most momentous thing in human life is the art of winning the soul to good or to evil. Blest are the men who acquire a good soul; if it be bad they can never be at rest, nor ever keep the same course two days together.'*[76]

HEKATE IN THE CHALDEAN ORACLES

In later antiquity, Hekate's role as intermediary became linked with the World Soul. In Plato's Philebus, Plato has Sokrates say

---

[75] Πλούταρχος *Ἠθικά Concerning the Face Which Appears in the Orb of the Moon* Chap. 28, 943C; trans. Harold Cherniss and William C. Helmbold, 1957, as found in the 1967 Loeb reprint entitled *Plutarch's Moralia Vol. XII*, Harvard Univ. Press [Cambridge MA]-William Heinemann [London] p. 201.

[76] (Διογένης Λαέρτιος *The Lives and Opinions of Eminent Philosophers*, Book 8.31, trans. by C. D. Yonge, 1828; Henry G. Bohn Publ. [London]).

that the souls of individual bodies are derived from that One which ensouls the body of the Kosmos - this soul is similar to, but fairer than, the souls of men. The idea of the World Soul is expanded upon in Plato's Timaeus.

The Chaldean Oracles appeared during the time of the Middle Platonic philosophers, and attempted to unite philosophy, religion and theurgy. Hekate had renewed prominence, being linked to the World Soul in Plato's Timaeus, whose form was a celestial X (Greek letter Chi). In the Timaeus, Plato describes two cosmic principles which are conjoined in the form of two intersecting circles, which, when looked at face on, make the form of the X (the Crossroads of Hekate). These he described as 'the Same' and 'the Different'. The Same and the Different are unified within the Soul. Later Platonic philosophers understood these principles as the Intelligible and Sensible realms – the realm of Unchanging Divinity and that of Changing mortality.

Plato says that the motion of the Different is the course of the planets, whilst leaving the explanation of the motion of The Same somewhat vague. Later writers, from Cicero to Manilius to Macrobius and beyond, who influenced the development of Platonic cosmology, link these circles to the circle of the Zodiac (the path of the planets) and the circle of the Milky Way, which cross in the sky. At the intersection of these two celestial circles are the heavenly gates. Hekate is the holder of the keys, she who has the keys to unlock and lock the heavenly gates, and also the Gates of Hades. The Crossroads of Hekate can be seen as the celestial X of the Gates of Heaven. Hekate is present wherever souls cross boundaries between life and death, and where the soul experiences the 'death and rebirth' of the mysteries. Depictions of the Eleusinian Mysteries in ancient art also show a torch in the form of an X, and Hekate carries two torches representing the two cosmic principles.

In the Chaldean Oracles and to the Middle Platonists, the Cosmic Soul was a multi-faceted intermediary between two worlds. The 'Forms' or 'Ideas' of the Intelligible realm were received by the Cosmic Soul, who in turn cast them onto Primal Matter, which then became the physical Universe. It is through the Cosmic Soul that the Cosmos is structured into its proper proportions and order. The Cosmic Soul is also the generator of individual souls. In the Philebus, Plato's Sokrates argues that if our bodies are derived from the greater body of the Cosmos, then logically our souls must be derived from the Cosmic Soul. Soul also encloses the Sensible (Physical) world, and is the receiver and transmitter of Ideas or Forms, giving proportion and harmony, and ensouling individual living beings. As the Cosmic Soul, Hekate became the intermediary between the Sensible and Intelligible realms, and it is at Her discretion that passage from one realm to another can occur. This intermediary role is an extension of her older role as Goddess of physical crossroads, doors, and liminal places.

Hekate's connection with the Moon in later antiquity is linked to Her role as intermediary, as the Moon is both a liminal point and a mediating entity, receiving the light of the Sun, and reflecting the light to the earth. Plutarch said that the Moon conducts down the warmth of the sun, and conducts upwards the exaltations of the Earth, refining them in the process. Thus, the Moon not only brings down the powers of the Heavens and the Intelligible realm, but can help to lift us to the Divine realm. Xenocrates describes the Moon as the intermediate layer in a three-tiered Universe. Xenocrates also placed the classes of daemones in the realm of the Moon, the daemones also being intermediate between Gods and men.

Hekate traditionally is the Queen of intermediary spirits, of phantoms and daemones. In the Living Orphic tradition, the intermediary daemones are represented by Her dogs, which are the agathes daemones, or good spirits which guide us and help us on our path, carry our prayers to the Gods, and can aid us in spiritual work. The daemones in Orphic and Platonic philosophy and mysticism also function to escort souls between realms.

As a goddess of boundaries and liminal places, as psychopomp, guide and intermediary, Hekate was also associated with a number of other deities, such as Hermes, who she is often invoked in conjunction with, with Artemis as the Goddess who aids in the transition of birth in the physical realm, and with Rhea, the Great Mother, who births the physical world. The Ideas of the Intelligible realm are given structure and harmony in the womb of Hekate, or Rhea, and then birthed into the physical Universe. She was also associated with the Roman Janus, another god of boundaries, as can be seen from Proclus's Hymn to Hekate, Janus and Zeus.

In this hymn, the first to be invoked is the Mother of the Gods, generally considered to be Rhea. Proclus says of Rhea that

> *'the cause of generation has proceeded from Her principle, having received the rank of mother among all the paternal orders and introducing the Demiurge before all the other Gods, the universal Demiurge and the inflexible safe-keeper.'*

He goes on to say:

> *'Concerning Rhea, the generative source, from whom all divine life, intellectual, spiritual and mundane, is generated, the Oracles speak as follows, 'Truly Rhea is the source and stream of blessed and intellectual (realities, Because She, the first in power, receives the birth of all beings in Her inexpressible womb and pours forth (this birth) on the All as it runs its course'.*

So, in Proclus' Hymn, Rhea, Hekate and Janus/Zeus are mentioned together: first the Mother, then the median principle of the World Soul and then the Father and Demiurge.

PROCLUS' HYMN TO HEKATE, JANUS AND ZEUS

'Hail, many-named Mother of the Gods, whose children are fair
Hail, mighty Hekate of the Threshold
And hail to you also Forefather Janus, Imperishable Zeus
Hail to you Zeus most high.
Shape the course of my life with luminous Light
And make it laden with good things,
Drive sickness and evil from my limbs.
And when my soul rages about worldly things,
Deliver me purified by your soul-stirring rituals.
Yes, give me your hand I pray
And reveal to me the pathways of divine guidance that I long for,
Then shall I gaze upon that precious Light
Whence I can flee the evil of our dark origin.
Yes, give me your hand I pray,
And when I am weary bring me to the haven of piety with your winds.
Hail, many-named mother of the Gods, whose children are fair
Hail, mighty Hekate of the Threshold
And hail to you also Forefather Janus, Imperishable Zeus,
Hail to you Zeus most high.'

In summary, Hekate is an important goddess who has many roles. She is the goddess of crossroads and thresholds, who holds the keys to the gates of Heaven and to Hades. She is a goddess who dwells in the darkness, but brings light, shedding light on and guiding us through the mysteries. As a goddess of thresholds, she is an intermediary between us and the gods, as an advocate, and leading us to virtue and to the divine light of the gods. She aids us through all transitions, as a goddess who holds the keys to the three worlds, but dwells in the "middle place", the intermediate between the unmanifest and the manifest. She is the goddess of the liminal, of boundaries, where paths and forces converge. She is honoured at the dark of the moon, in that space where one lunar month has ended and the next is about to begin. Hekate can guide us through and help us to understand the mysteries. On a more mundane level, Hekate guards the threshold of our homes, along with Hermes and Apollon Prostaterius (Apollon standing before the door) and Apollon Horion (Apollon of the limits, of boundaries).

PENTASPENDIA OFFERING TO HEKATE

<u>Homeric Hymn to Hestia</u> – light candle

<u>Purify water with flame</u>

<u>Asperging with water and bunches of rosemary.</u>

<u>Orphic Hymn to Hekate:</u>

> *I call Enodian Hecate, lovely dame,*
> *Of earthly, wat'ry, and celestial frame,*
> *Sepulchral, in a saffron veil array'd,*
> *Leas'd with dark ghosts that wander thro' the shade;*
> *Persian, unconquerable huntress hail!*
> *The world's key-bearer never doom'd to fail;*
> *On the rough rock to wander thee delights,*
> *Leader and nurse be present to our rites*
> *Propitious grant our just desires success,*
> *Accept our homage, and the incense bless.*

<u>Begin Chant IAΩ</u>

<u>Chanting to HEKATE SOTEIRA</u>
<u>Libation</u>

As we are chanting, people take it in turn to pour libations/offerings to Hekate of Olive oil, Almond milk, Honey water, Wine, and Rose Water.

<u>Pore-Breathing meditation</u> – connecting with the World Soul

Sit in a meditative posture and relax your body and mind. Visualise yourself sitting in the centre of a universe that is filled with light, a light that has some substance to it, like a radiant white plasma. Imagine that this white light is pulsing with energy that is radiating outwards in all directions and is also pushing in on you from all directions, trying to expand itself into you.

Now imagine your body is hollow and empty, filled with the blackness of empty space.

Inhale slowly and let the vital force expand into you from all directions. Initially you may see a white light and energy coming in through your nose as you breathe in, but remember that we breathe not only through our nose and mouth, but also through every pore of our bodies. Begin to see the white light entering your body through every pore, absorbing it like a sponge.

At the fullest point of inhalation, feel the energy totally filling your body, and see your body glowing brightly, filled with the energy. Allow a natural pause to experience this, but do not hold your breath.

Exhale and push all of the radiant white light and energy back out through your skin with your breath. At the end of the exhalation, you should again be hollow and completely empty.

Repeat this process 10 times.

Now we ask Hekate for guidance on our paths, to be the best that we can and achieve *Areti*:

ὦ φωσφόρ' Ἑκάτη, Ἑκάτη, πέμπε φάσματ' εὐμενῆ.
O phosphor Hekate, Hekate, pempe phasmat evmeni
O torch-bearing Hekate, send visions that are favourable!

Quiet meditation to commune with Hekate and ask for Her guidance.

Μακαρ οστισ ευδαιμων
Τελετασ θεων ειδωσ
Βιοταν αγιστευει και
Θιασευεται φυχαν
Εν ορεσσι Βακχευων

Makar hostis efdaimon
Teletas theon eidos
Viotan agistevei kai
Thisaveti psychon
En orresi Vakcheaion

Blessed are they who, being fortunate,
And knowing the rites of the Gods
Keep their souls pure
And are initiated
Into the Rites of Bacchus

Evohe, Evohe, Evohe

Hail Hekate, Soteira, Blessed Maid
Embodiment of Arete
Hail Hekate, Soul of the World,
Advocate, and Queen of Mystery

Hail Dionysos, Lord of the Mysteries,
Who gives the Aithir of Wine
Hail Hera, Mother of Life,
Hail Zefs, King Divine
May we receive Your Divine blessings wherever we go
Yaenito, Yaenito, Yaenito, Yaenito!

Sources

Fritz Graf & Sarah Iles Johnson, Ritual Texts for the Afterlife, 2007, Routledge London & New York

Sarah Iles Johnson, Hekate Soteira, 1990, American Philosophical Association, Scholars Press, Atlanta

Thomas Taylor tr., Hymn of Orpheus, 2007, Forgotten Books

www.hellenicgods.org

www.theoi.com

Kore vs. Crone:
History, Transcendence & Respect

Contributed by Marcel Schrei, Germany

A frequent occurrence in the Hekatean community seems to be the controversy surrounding whether Hekate may be called a 'Crone'. Usually there are three parties involved: the 'She told me/I deeply feel she is a Crone-ers', the 'All ancient texts call her Maiden-ers' and the 'Why should we care-ers'. Whenever I witness these disputes, usually online, I feel really annoyed. This is not because of any one of these points of view, or the mere existence of these quarrels, as I do believe that a good respectful talk about theological differences generally is a benefit for all. What really ticks me off is the way these arguments are led by some participants: they show a deep lack of respect, not only towards each other, but also to our predecessors and even Our Lady herself. The last time I started to rant on that subject I was asked: What on earth is this Maiden/Crone fuss all about? So, let's start with a little historical overview. (Note: I am not proficient in Greek, neither ancient nor modern, and only rudimentary in Latin, therefore this work relies on translations and secondary sources.)

KORE: AN ANTIQUE VIEW?

Let's talk about the sources from antiquity. Was Hekate called a Maiden, κόρη?

According to the sources I have reviewed, Hekate's age usually wasn't mentioned. Hesiod's 8th century BCE Theogony gives an account of her ancestry and domains but doesn't state her age – except the fact that she was a member of the older dynasty of gods, the Titans. Approximately one century later in the Homeric Hymn to Demeter, Hekate appears twice; first helping Demeter in finding the abducted Persephone, later as Persephone's attendant and guide, but again her age is no issue. An interesting point here is that Κόρη, maiden or daughter, was in fact an epithet of Persephone with whom Hekate was later sometimes conflated or confused.

What can be said about the surviving depictions of Hekate from antiquity? The same as those other goddesses and mythological women: she was depicted as an adult female human of indefinable age, whether as a statue, on vases, on coins, wall paintings or reliefs. This could be due to the peculiar aesthetics of ancient Greek art, but there is no time to go into detail here.

Around the 5th century BCE, Hekate became first conflated with Artemis by Aeschylus in his play 'The Supplicants'. Artemis, goddess of hunting, sister of Apollon and cousin of Hekate, was generally known as a maiden goddess. Could this conflation, which continued thereafter, be an origin of the 'Hekate as Maiden' point of view? In his 462 BCE Pythian Odes, Pindar calls Hekate 'red-footed Maiden'. In sources and inscriptions mentioning Hekate over the next several centuries I found no trace of her being called Maiden until late antiquity. Around c.2nd CE, Hekate was explicitly attributed to be a κόρη in her Orphic Hymn. At around the same time, the Chaldean Oracles call her a *'virgin of varied forms.'* In at least two spells from around the 4th CE found in the Greek Magic Papyri (PGM) the magician is advised to make a picture of Hekate having (among other attributes) the head of a maiden. So, in antiquity we find no trace of Hekate being called a Crone, but she is named a Maiden. Additionally, Hekate was frequently called, or conflated with, the Mother Goddesses Kybele or Rhea. In Proclos Diadochus' 5th century CE Hymn to Hekate, Janus refers to her as 'Mother of Gods', as does the PGM 'Prayer to Selene for any spell', whilst Neoplatonic commentaries to the Chaldean Oracles explicitly equate her with the Mother Goddesses Rhea and Isis. Circe, Medea, and even the notorious sea monster Skylla are said to be her children, although this could be metaphoric. In short, if an age was attributed to Hekate at all, it seems to be ambivalent: Maiden or Mother.

CRONE: A 'MODERN' VIEW?

After 60 CE Lucan in Pharsalia tells us about the worship of Hekate by the witches from Thessaly and how they called to her in their necromantic rites. The emphasis here is more to show necromancy and magic in general as outlandish practices, as Lucan's witch Erictho calls to several primordial and chthonic forces besides Hekate. The PGM also connect her with necromantic rites. Still, she is not called Crone in any of these sources, but they might have fuelled the Christian writers' tendency to perceive Hekate exclusively as a goddess of evil witchcraft and necromancy. Please note that magic and witchcraft were considered evil and criminal by Christians as well as Greek and Roman Pagans– especially when performed in secret outside of the official cults.

After the rise of Christianity, we have to take a leap in time to 1606 CE. Here, Hekate appears in William Shakespeare's play Macbeth as mistress (possibly, but not explicitly stated, goddess) of the witches. While in the early modern period witches were at times, but not exclusively, depicted as old and 'ugly' (see Albrecht Dürer's 1500's print 'Witch' riding backwards on a goat) no age or other appearance of any of the witches is stated in the play. Most interestingly, the witches in Macbeth do not worship Satan either.

It was Aleister Crowley in his 1929 novel Moonchild who first used the term Crone for Hekate, although this was (misogynistic child of the Victorian Era that he was) in a derogatory way: *'Hekate is the Crone, the woman past all hope of motherhood, her soul black with envy and hatred of happier mortals'*. This is obviously not the Crone as 'old wise woman' most have in mind today.

In 1938 the ceremonial magician Dion Fortune, in her novel The Sea Priestess, started the notorious and oft-quoted claim that 'All goddesses are one Goddess'. We should note that The Sea Priestess is not a scientific or theological work but a novel, just as Crowley's Moonchild was. Furthermore, Fortune herself was no pagan - her magical order 'Fraternity of the Inner Light' was explicitly Christian, which Fortune's successors in that order explicitly emphasised.

In 1948 the construct of the 'Triple Goddess' with different ages emerged for the first time in Robert Graves's 'The White Goddess'. Triads of goddesses like the Fates, the Norns or the Gallo-Roman Matrones (Mothers) as well as our Hekate Triformis appeared earlier, but here, for the first time, different ages are attributed to the different aspects. Graves draws from a huge bunch of sources, including Fortune, Crowley and Sir James Frazer's Golden Bough. Frazer states among other claims the existence of a duo of harvest goddesses as mother and daughter. Graves brings all these mentioned sources together and applies them to the goddess Ceridwen. I have to admit that I lost track amidst reading The White Goddess when Graves started to throw a tree alphabet into his cauldron of information, but I could not find him calling Hekate or any other deity a 'Crone' aspect of his triple muse.

In addition to Crowley, Fortune and Graves, we may also recount Dr. Margaret Murray's 1921 and 1931 works on the supposed 'witch cult' and what Gerald Gardner and his co-workers and successors made out of it from the 1940s onwards (Ronald Hutton's 1999 book 'The Triumph of the Moon' gives details on this interesting subject of religious history). Interestingly 'The Goddess' in Gardner's Book of Shadows is always spoken of as 'Mother' and the High Priestess is supposed to 'recognise that youth is necessary to the representative of the

Goddess, so she will retire gracefully in favour of a younger woman' in the 1961 'Old Laws', found in the aforementioned Book of Shadows. So, there's not even a trace of the Crone in the origin of the movement that became most influential in contemporary paganism.

It seems that the women's empowerment and spirituality movements of the 1960s later took inspiration from these sources, and the Maiden-Mother-Crone concept came into the hearts and minds of the wider pagan community, with Hekate's name commonly being attributed to the Crone aspect. Unfortunately, I could not find out exactly who came up with this affiliation.

DIVINE NATURE: TRANSCENDING HUMAN PERCEPTION?

So, is Hekate now a Maiden or a Crone? Or is she the Maiden-Mother-Crone Triple Goddess?

I think it is a bit complicated. Let me sum up: in the last 2800 years people have had very different and individual experiences with Our Lady. She revealed herself alternately and independently as Maiden, as Mother and most recently as Crone, but never as all of them at the same time. We have to note the following too: all we know about Hekate, be it from antiquity or modern, comes from human experience. As human beings we have the limited perception of our body's senses, we think in our human 'categories' according to our human experience in life.

It is my understanding that Our Lady - like any deity - transcends the boundaries of the limited human perception. She appears in individual shapes to answer individual needs. She does what she wants and doesn't care about human categories of age or form. This perception is neither new nor limited to Hekate or Greek culture: Hesiod's Theogony states that Hekate gives and withdraws Her blessings according to Her own will. We have seen Her manifold perception throughout history, be it age or form (such as triple-formed, animal-headed). The Homeric Hymn to Demeter tells us how Demeter in Eleusis disguises herself as an old woman and reveals herself later in her true divine form. Zeus is said to be a shapeshifter, as is Odin in Norse mythology. The 4th century CE pagan writer Sallustius states that 'the gods are unchanged by human actions'.

After years of privately studying and comparing religions I have come to this conclusion: It's all about the connection between the deity and the individual devotee.

THE DEAL: THREE FACES OF RESPECT

One may ask now: "If it is all about individual relationship and personal revelation, why should I care about history or other people's feelings?" My answer is: Out of respect! As with many things Hekatean, this comes threefold: Respect towards our ancestors, respect towards Our Lady, and respect towards one another.

In the pagan community we usually emphasise respect towards our ancestors, be they bloodline or spiritual. To me, this includes a lot of respect towards their religious feelings and practices. While from our contemporary point of view we might object to some of these (such as killing animals as part of offering rites) we should still be aware that these were an important part of our predecessors' everyday life. We have strong feelings towards our religious views and should assume our ancestors had strong feelings towards theirs. I'm not saying that we should adopt every detail our ancestors believed and do so just for the sake of it, but we should be aware of history. All of this should also apply to other cultures, no matter whether contemporary or ancient.

Also, as Our Lady chose to reveal herself in the various ways she did in history, we should assume that she did so for a reason. The ancient texts and archaeological evidence are our starting point and guideline on our individual paths towards a deeper understanding of Our Lady in the past and present. What she may show us in the future we cannot know. Ignoring er revelations of the past, however contradictory they may appear at first glance, feels highly disrespectful towards the very goddess we worship. I cannot emphasise this enough and recommend everyone study as much of the classical texts regarding Hekate as possible.

SUMMARY: "ALL I'M ASKIN'..."

To me, Hekate is neither Kore nor Crone and yet is both at the same time. She is ageless and timeless. Her varied forms can inspire us to research as much as possible about her origins and dive deeply into her contemporary mysteries to improve our own personal relationship with her. I am very aware that my point of view here might be controversial. That's OK. I don't want to tell anyone what or what not to believe; I endorse diversity in faith and religion. As I said in the introduction, I believe that discussing religious differences can help us see beyond our own respective noses.

So perhaps we all could profit from a little respect.

SOURCES

Sorita d'Este (editor), Hekate Her Sacred Fires, 2010, Avalonia

Sorita d'Este & David Rankine, Hekate Liminal Rites, 2009, Avalonia

Sir James Frazer, The Golden Bough, 1922, 1993 edition, Wordsworth Reference

The Gardnerian Book of Shadows, 1949-1961, as compiled and chronologically sorted by Aidan Kelly ~1995, found on http://www.sacred-texts.com/pag/gbos/

Fritz Graf, Magic in the Ancient World (I used the German edition: Gottesnähe und Schadenszauber – Die Magie in der griechisch-römischen Antike, 1996, C.H.Beck

Robert Graves, The White Goddess, 1948, 1966 edition, Farrar, Straus and Giroux

Hesiod, Theogony, ~ c8th BCE, various translations

Homeric Hymn to Demeter, ~ C7th BCE, cited on http://www.stoa.org/diotima/anthology/demeter.shtml

Ronald Hutton, The Triumph of the Moon, 1999, Oxford University Press

Sarah Iles Johnston, Hekate Soteira, 1990, Scholars Press

Thomas Lautwein, Hekate die dunkle Göttin, 2009, Edition Roter Drache

Kaatryn MacMorgan-Douglas, The Ethical Eclectic, 2007, Covenstead Press

Kaatryn MacMorgan-Douglas, Wicca 333, 2003, 2007 edition, Covenstead Press

Orphic Hymn to Hekate, ~ C2nd CE, various translations

Sallustius, About the Gods and the World, 362/363 CE, cited in Gerald Gardner, The Meaning of Witchcraft, 1959, 2000 edition, I-H-O Books

Tara Sanchez, The Temple of Hekate, 2011, Avalonia

William Shakespeare, Macbeth, ~1606, cited on http://theshakespeareproject.com/macbeth/macbeth-1-1.html

Lawrence Sutin, Do What Thou Wilt: A Life of Aleister Crowley, 2000, St Martin's Press, cited on en.wikipedia.org/wiki/Aleister_Crowley

https://en.wikipedia.org/wiki/Triple_Goddess_%28Neopaganism%29

Hekate Rexchthon: Raising up the Goddess

Contributed by Orryelle Defenestrate-Bascule

'Hekate Rexchthon' at Le Chalet Crepuscule

In a small but potent patch of forest, near the tiny village of Harsin in the verdant Ardennes area of southern Belgium, stands an imposing 2.3 metre-tall (7.5ft) statue of the goddess Hekate in Her form of *Rexchthon*: She who erupts up out of the earth, from the depths of the Underworld.

This is not only Her title, it is the actual process of Her coming into being in Her current manifestation in clay and metal, bones, fabrics, hair and wood. Her base is formed from the twisting serpentine roots of a mighty tree-trunk, some which still reach claw-like back into the soil, others rising up like cobras ready to strike. Threads of varied hue and texture twine about these roots, some hidden dangling below, others visible through the holes in layers of lace, frayed decaying and moss-green at the bottom, some still white and ornamentally pristine at the waistline of Her skirts. These threads are sacred, they have been tied woven and twisted with prayers and intentions by various visitors to the Goddess' woodland shrine, mostly during group rituals at Lammas/Lughnasadh and Beltane gatherings there.

Above the waistline of lace She is bare, Her earthen abdomen and six arms exposed to the elements. White paint peels in textured layers like skin from the more classically flesh-toned clay beneath. Above, Her three heads look out as three worlds, faces sometimes serene, sometimes intense and even foreboding according to the play of light from the dappled foliage over their features (or perhaps Her diverse expressions indicative of something more). Several years after Her initial creation/eruption, She ages well appearing somehow half-dead and half-alive, Gothically ghostly in moonlight, more solid in daylight hours and especially ethereal yet manifest in the twilight hours, the liminal Crossroad Goddess's special time of *in-between* -life and death, day and night, underworld and overworld. The sunsets at this powerful place are often spectacular, especially at the end of long summer days when the four pine trunks before Her (surrounding the stone altar) glow red-golden; and in the ambiguous Autumn, the twilight of the year also. It is thus that I named the place (in the language of the locals) *Le Chalet Crepuscule*. Before erupting into manifest form She was perceived astrally beneath the ground by I, Her sculptor. I call myself this as I did the work of crafting Her into form, yet I feel I cannot claim full credit for this creation except as a vessel - She made Herself through my hands, although of course they did have the dexterity (or should I say sinisterity, considering I am primarily left-handed) required for the job.

It was a Lammas (August harvest festival) full moon, the first I celebrated there in 2017, with the land's then-owner Kolja. After contemplating the idea for a few months after he'd told me of his intention to sell the place (I'd been there a few years earlier) I had only just decided that I would definitely buy the land and chalet thereon from him. Having forsaken my homeland of Australia for its lack of artistic heritage (within modern western civilisation there) and waning sub/culture, I had been looking for a European base for a few years, mostly in Portugal and also considering other countries where land is cheap, such as Italy. Belgium is not generally such a cheap country so I had not considered it until I was offered this option, which was surprisingly affordable - due to being off-grid and also being purchased from a friend who wanted another magician, rather than just anybody, to inherit the place.

We began our ritual at dusk, the twilight time significant to both the HermAphroditic ChAOrder of the Silver Dusk I was about to initiate him into, and to the Crepuscular place. I cast the circle, and we chanted the chakra tones together. Then we proceeded with the initiation, which went smoothly considering we'd had to expand the physically-cleared space of the circle to include some spiralling and dervish-dancing. The ritual ended with a visit to the astral temple of the Silver Dusk. My journey there was most interesting, beginning with the sensation that the astral space I was in was actually literally *under* the ground of the altar area where we were sitting. It's always a journey down into the earth, but this time felt much more localised and almost physical. I won't write here much of my experiences in the astral temple as it is for ChAOrder members; except where they are relevant to this essay in relation the Hekate statue:

I saw Kolja in the astral temple and we had a brief and somewhat vague exchange in which I gave him a key. The irony of that in relation to the land occurred to me and he grinned and gave me a key in exchange - physical for astral temple?

Afterwards, I remembered that when clearing the space around the altar for the ritual, he had unearthed an old physical key to the chalet from under a rock there. I guess the Keys recalled Hekate to my subconscious (or I to Hers?) as I'd received one from Her once in the depths of the temple. For She was there before me, a little larger than human size; then suddenly She moved upwards and in Her wake was a swathe of twining lace wound through the branching roots of Her skirts. I became entangled in these and went up with Her, as She erupted up out of the surface of the earth. The vision remained after I returned to the physical (for the eruption brought me back to my body) - perhaps She would be there on the land, a gargantuan statue similar in form to the small bronze Hekate Chthonia I had crafted years ago, but rather than Her skirts being cast from tangled tree-roots and lace into bronze, they would be formed of the original materials, on a far greater scale...

I'd planned to make a statue of Ardennia, the Goddess of the Ardennes, a fairly obscure Celtic deity as the first statue there, as She was the local forest Goddess of that geographical area. Cernunnos was also a priority, as I had felt the presence of the great Antlered One strongly there. But when Chthonic Hekate erupted out of the earth and I saw Her standing there in roots-lace-and-clay glory, I knew She needed to be made first -I certainly wasn't going to argue with the Dark Lady!

The need for a physical Temple for the Silver Dusk became paramount, a place where magicians, witches and artists can gather, ritualize and create together. Just a few weeks later I signed the papers to purchase Le Chalet Crepuscular and the small patch of land it is on - ironically, on the day I was returning to Australia (my homeland). I knew that when I returned to Europe everything would be different with such a base.

Upon first arriving in Belgium from Australia the following year (2018) I was so jet-lagged and sleep-deprived that I left my violin in the overhead racks of the train on the way to my new chalet in the Ardennes. The next day I was trying to locate it for hours with google-translate and skype calls from the nearby village bar, really hoping it wasn't gone with my first gig in Belgium (all the way back in Antwerp, 3 hours away) in just a few days. It was a communications nightmare with all the different unfamiliar languages: Dutch, French and even Luxembourgish as that tiny country is at the end of the train-line I was on. That night I prayed fervently to Hermes at the stone altar at le Chalet Crepuscule, for the swift safe return of my lost violin, and the next day to my great relief I found with much less phone hassle that it was in the small town of Arlon, the last stop in Belgium before Luxembourg >phew< When I went to pick it up I discovered a huge metal statue of Hermes next to the train-station. Hail Thrice Greatest Hermes! Thrice Greatest Hermes! Thrice Greatest Hermes! O Mighty fleet-footed patron of Travellers!

I mention this as the strong relationship between Hermes and Hekate - as Lord and Lady of the Crossroads, both psychopomps - is one which has continued to be central to my connection with the land of Le Chalet Crepuscule; and indeed the feather-fledged One is intrinsic to the strange tale I am about to unfold...

It was only a few weeks after my return to Belgium that, while wandering through the narrow patch of forest behind my property, I saw on the edge of an adjacent field the bottom half of a severed tree that had an incredible array of roots twisting and twining around each other in a most serpentine fashion. It was undoubtedly the base of the Hekate statue, just as in my vision. Embedded in mud, it took some effort to free it, then a few days later with the aid of Kola's father Frank who lived in a village nearby, we half-dragged and half-wheeled it together (he has a strength and fitness belying his age) through a vast field - while thunder and lightning heralded the onset of a great storm - and hoisted it with difficulty into the back of his trailer just as the tumultuous rain began. He drove it back around to my land via the road and we somehow got it into my little patch of forest, where it sat for weeks drying in the sun, with me gradually peeling away rotting bark from the marvellous morass of entangled roots. When this base was well-coated with an anti-rot lacquer, I placed it in the exact spot where I had seen Her rise from the Underworld, which was perfect in its orientation to the stone altar (already created by Kolja and used for years before my arrival) and the general energetic flow of the land. There was a shorter but wider tree-stump (just a few inches tall) in just the right place, which provided a stable base. Once the roots were in place - some arching upwards like rising cobras, some clawing back into the dirt - I noticed a very young oak behind it. It was only the size of a narrow branch, with a few definite leaves sprouting, but what was significant is that it had only grown vertically about 15cm, then veered off horizontally (with a very slight diagonal upwards) for about 60cms, towards the place where the statue was now forming. It was as if it had already known for a few years She was coming and had begun to grow towards Her.

Now years later, it's a little larger and I have begun to wind its top twigs and leaves into Her lacy skirts. It is my fervent hope that this little oak will continue to grow with and on Her, so that eventually rather than periodically replenishing the oak leaves on Her garland of serpent skins, She will be wreathed with living growing oak leaves!

Crafting the statue was incredibly challenging. I had never made a sculpture this big before. The closest was the one other clay statue (rather than figurine) of Kali, that I had made in Australia on return from a long trip to India. I deeply missed having temples to pray at, so decided to make one, and began with the statue! She was extremely difficult, with four arms and a height about equivalent to mine. Having failed to consider the structural necessities for such a scale, as they are not needed for smaller clay works, the epic project was rescued by my friend Tas in the last few weeks before Her debut in the 'Loom of Lila' ritual dance theatre production. He welded together a metal skeleton which enabled all the clay pieces I'd assembled to actually stand up.

Having learnt something from this experience, I approached this one differently with a structural frame at the beginning, but there were also the added challenges that She was even larger (I only came up to Her lower armpit) and with six rather than four arms, plus three heads and necks! Also, I had nobody with welding skills or equipment to help, instead creating a more basic infrastructure by shafting a central thick metal 'spine' into the top of the tree-stump (at least such a base was sturdier and more manageable than regular legs), then three smaller lighter metal rods through holes near the top of this spine to form the mainframe for the arms. It was all very experimental but seemed a solid enough start... Nevertheless, the process remained ambiguous - I was basically just working it out as I went and made many big mistakes. There were times of pure frustration, where after pieces fell apart, I became totally consternated as to how it was possible to realise the grand vision on a practical level. But every time something like this happened, there would be some magical synchronicity which gave me fresh hope, some cosmic indication that She was with me, creating Herself through my hands and that, regardless of my knowledge or skills to succeed with such an ambitious endeavour, I somehow actually could not fail.

I had to make many separate pieces then work out how to join them together on the framework and base: each arm and face a different piece of the giant puzzle, and the torso in two pieces, back and front with even some joining side panels. The main reason for this was a lack of a kiln large enough to fire anything bigger. I doubt there would have been a ceramic kiln big enough for the whole top half of the statue in all of Belgium, but I was also constrained by lack of a car or licence to fire them locally. It had actually been one of the interesting synchronicities with the locality that had helped confirm it was the right place, that just 20 minutes walk away was a small community called La Gatte D'Or, which is Old French for 'The Golden Goat', named after a local legend and a small ancient relic found quite near my chalet of an actual gold figurine of a goat! That this community's presence so close-by was particularly synchronous, in that there was nothing much else in the area other than farm-land and forest, and what's more, they sometimes had ceramic classes for children from nearby villages, and so they had a ceramic kiln there I could use (even at a discount price once I got to know them!). It would have been an amusing and odd image should anyone ever have seen me (only donkeys in the adjacent field had the pleasure) walking through the thin wedge of forest behind my land with under each of my arms a much larger ceramic arm of Hekate, with gnarly hands and long claws, to take them to be fired at La Gatte D'Or.

Of course, with all these separate pieces I still needed to somehow keep track of the cohesion of the whole, so I had them all laid out horizontally on a large outdoor table, even joining some together for a while for continuity then breaking them apart later when semi-dry. I found some of my sawn firewood logs to be perfect to wrap sheets of flattened clay around creating the hollow infrastructure for the limbs, then removing them when the resultant clay tubes were dry enough to support their own weight and be shaped into a more particular resemblance to over-sized arms. The torso, faces and particularly the triple-neck were trickier, requiring frameworks hand-shaped from metal mesh. The stuff I had from an art shop didn't seem sturdy enough for the big abdomen, but after a long session of chanting Hekate's different epithets I suddenly realised a wire mesh rubbish-bin I had was stronger and actually the right size and - with some minor semi-flattening - approximately the right shape! This kind of improvisation was constant and often surprisingly effective. Had I found a course on how to create structurally-sound giant statues I may not have discovered such effective innovations. Often, I would be just grabbing whatever was around while I worked - suddenly needing a prop even as a wet clay part was beginning to droop, I would find pieces of wood, rocks, rubbish, odd scraps which I would adjust and include for temporary support on the fly...

There were of course mishaps too with such an approach! The worst accident was when I decided I needed to work on the abdomen with it set up vertically on the frame and tree-stump base (rather than horizontally on the outdoor workbench) to ascertain how it was going to come together as a whole, particularly joining the sides front and back. Even anatomically it was tricky, to work out how six, rather than two, arms slotted into ribs and triple shoulder-blades believably. The wire bin-frame slid easily over the spinal pole, and I figured the front and back clay pieces, though only half-formed, were now dry enough to sit upright on the now vertical infrastructure. I had a live model at this stage of the process, and it seemed perfect timing, as referencing how her body fit together from different angles allowed me to bridge the gaps in the abdominal pieces, as well as refine the details of each. It was all going well and looked good for a while working just on the back, taking it off again then putting up and working on the front. I could support the large pieces of semi-dry clay myself as I worked with my other hand, sometimes even my chest, though I was mostly standing precariously on the tree-roots rather than ground to reach up. Then I needed to bridge front and back with sides, so I propped the back to the frame with large forked sticks and rocks at their base while I held the front on. At one stage there was an almost-collapse, but the model ran in in time to grab the other side before it completely fell off. After a few hours however, my modelling friend had to leave for Brussels. I continued the work for another hour or so, and it all seemed solid enough by now with the side sections smoothed into back and front to hold it all together. I was feeling quite happy with the progress and cohesive form, even though I knew I would have to soon break it apart again to remove from the vertical structure and have the pieces fired. But then, when I stepped back for a moment to view the results from a few different angles, cracks suddenly started to form. I rushed in and up onto the roots (which made the whole thing wobble slightly), grabbed the front piece just in time before it could fall off. But the props slipped at the back, and with less hands than Her I could only watch in horror as the entire back piece with its intricately sculpted spine, musculature and six shoulder-blades folded up accordion-like as it slid down and landed in a squelchy pile of formlessness in the leaves and sticks. Fuck!!

My devotion got me through moments like these. I was constantly chanting or singing Hekate's names and epithets every day while I worked, and the entire process was a deep devotional ritual to Her. The back, somehow, turned out even better the second time.

At some stage during the process of creation when things weren't flowing so well, it occurred to me that I had not made a proper offering to Hermes in gratitude for His aid in locating my violin. So, I performed a ritual to the Lord of the Crossroads, giving him an egg, eloquent prayers and other such things the God of communications favours. I was working hard on the statue for many hours almost every day, only having short breaks when I had to go to civilisation for a few days here and there (visiting friends in cities, gigs etc.). And of course, where magic is involved, it is a fine line between obsession and possession. I was working towards a self-imposed deadline, trying to get the gargantuan statue finished in time for the first Lammas/Lughnasadh Gathering there (August full moon 2018) which had been promoted online as the official unveiling of the Hekate statue. There were times towards the end where in the middle of hectic work it occurred to me that there was perhaps a degree of obsessive insanity going on, in that considering the place is remote by European standards and wasn't yet known, effectively I was working my arse off to present it to just between probably 13 to 18 of my friends! The realisation did not stop me. I am of a nature, especially with devotional projects, that when I say I will do something by a certain time I will somehow do so regardless of setbacks. But the biggest last-minute disaster was yet to occur...

It resulted from the peril of doing new work in a country where you don't yet know the language/s. I'd been buying clay at the beginning from an art-shop in Antwerp and foolishly didn't ask for details, simply got the cheapest type (needing so much of it) that looked like the right kind of consistency and taking it home - one 10kg bag in each of my bike's saddlebags riding from the nearest train-station. It was only when I later (on a subsequent visit to Antwerp) asked about the correct firing temperature that the art-shop assistant looked at the Flemish label and told me it was so cheap because it was a mixed bag of leftovers of various different types, and generally considered only 'practice clay' - Ffuuuck!!

I had in the meantime found out from the good people at La Gatte d'Or about a bulk clay place much nearer to my home and went there with Frank, filling his car with many bags of a coarse grained clay suitable for large works. Only the hands and some forearms had been made with the mixed clay, but there were six of the latter and each beautifully detailed with fingers shaped to hold Her different tools. I continued on with the work hoping it would all still somehow be ok. Due to the slow drying of large pieces, firing was done with just enough time (I hoped!) to put all the pieces together before people arrived. There was a drought that August in Belgium. Unusual temperatures for the region and during the last week before Lammas full moon the usually-lush land felt parched and oppressive. I was hot and bothered, still working but wondering how people were even going to enjoy the gathering in such conditions.

'Hekate Rexchthon' at Le Chalet Crepuscule

I got the last pieces back from firing just a few days before the gathering. Well, four of Her six hands had exploded in the kiln due to the mixed clay - could have been worse, but only a little! Two were repairable with epoxy glue, sticking fingers back on etc., but two were just piles of shares and fragments, impossible three-dimensional jigsaw puzzles. After some raging disappointment I eventually realised it was actually a blessing in disguise (as were many of my mishaps): there was no way to make, and especially fire, new hands in time so I simply had to let go of an aspect of the work for the time being. I realised I could just present Her with four arms for the 16 people coming to Lammas, and add the other two arms with new hands later. This felt much better, as I was exhausted and struggling to get all Her arms to fit on in the right places and angles anyway... As if to affirm my decision and surrender, there was a sudden draught of cooling rain. It only lasted an hour or so but afterwards the land felt refreshed and habitable again. I fell to my knees in gratitude to Hekate Soteria.

When the first guests arrived, I was still up a rickety wooden ladder applying some quick-dry cement to keep an arm in place. Another was propped precariously on a Dr-Suess-like wyrdly angled stack of diverse decorative chairs and pieces of wood with epoxy glue drying. There was a black cloth half-draped across some trees in front of Her in half-arsed concealment for the great unveiling the next day, but of course my friends just came behind it to greet me anyway!

And so it was that the Hekate Rexchthon statue was there for the first Gathering at Le Chalet Crepuscule. The semi-finished version was all that was needed, but it *was* needed. She still looked rough and raw at that stage, heads a bit too high on Her shoulders, four arms wobbling in the wind, unsmoothed joins - but at night with 'wasfakkels' lit (it had taken me a while to find 'wax torches' in Antwerp) She still looked suitably primal. Her potent presence in the group ritual set the tone for many more to come. Participants had brought sacred threads to weave with their prayers into Her skirts as requested, which are layers of lace from which Her serpentine roots emerge. After Lammas I was able to work on the statue at a more measured pace again, making new hands, taking off Her heads to shorten the neck and shoulder fitting, refining and decorating. She was complete just before I left for Australia again, this time for just a few months as my base was in Europe now.

During this re-creation/refinement of the statue I became a bit anxious about the costs involved. I'd anticipated all the clay and firing costs, but there were so many unexpected extras to bring it all together cohesively: quick-dry cement, lots of expensive epoxy glue and putty, expandable foam to fill the arms, paint... It'd been about 600 euros by now and still going. Of course I wouldn't hold back on the expenses, whatever the Goddess required for the completion of Her manifestation. But having recently spent most of my savings on the land and needing more money to live here than in Australia, I did wonder how I was going to make another gargantuan statue the next year. As soon as these concerns arose, I suddenly discovered one day a considerable sum of money had appeared mysteriously in my account, the only indication of its source being an unknown 3-letter code and that it seemed to be from my bank itself. So I Googled the code and it led me to a news article about how Australia's Westpac bank had not been clear about their Foreign Transaction Fees. Someone had taken them to court and now they were refunding thousands of customers. For me it was quite a lot of money because I had been travelling so much in recent years and always taking out money in all different countries. As He presides over both commerce and travel, this seemed a pretty sure sign that Hermes was listening to my prayers. What really clinched it though was the amount was almost exactly the cost of crafting the statue, times two. So the next one was already covered too. Hail Thrice Greatest Hermes! Thrice Greatest Hermes! Thrice Greatest Hermes!

After several ritual gatherings and other occasional visitors Her skirts are well adorned. Offerings lie amidst the moss and leaves Her serpents twine through, talismans dangle from some of these roots. As new layers form some of the old ones begin to decompose in the elements, a beautiful organic process befitting of a Goddess of life and death, and the liminal spaces betwixt. As I write these lines I am preparing for the first Samhain Gathering (2021) here, which will feature the beginnings of a Labyrinth installation woven with string through the trees. As the central Weaver, threads extend out into the paths from Her lacy skirts, a natural extension of the first rituals with Her. The stone altar before Her (at which I chant almost every dusk I am there) between four great pines, sits at the central axis of the Labyrinth. On the other side of this Crossroads now sits the clay visage of Hermes, grinning winged head atop a pile of rocks, the traditional Herm at which offerings were (and still are) left for the God of travellers; and indeed, for travellers themselves.

The Numbers of Hekate

Contributed by Larry Phillips, Kansas USA

Before we delve into the subject of precise and discrete symbolism, it is important to note that in the *Chaldean Oracles*, Hekate governs the working of all symbols. As the Cosmic Soul, situated between the intelligible and sensible worlds, she both separates and connects. It is by Hekate's power that an image or object in the sensible, material world is linked to an immaterial essence or power in the intelligible, spiritual world. She governs the path from one to the other, making the magical use of symbols and sacred words possible.

HEKATE AND NUMBERS

Like the working of symbols, Hekate as the Cosmic Soul is associated with all numbers and even the concept of number and measurement. In Plato's *Timaeus*, the Cosmic or World Soul is said to be composed of Number and all numbers, because it is through numbers that the Cosmic Soul organises and orders the manifest world. The Soul (*Psyche*) receives the Ideas or Forms from the divine mind (the *Nous*) and converts them into mathematical principles which are then projected onto matter to construct the world. Numbers are to the Cosmic Soul, as the Ideas or Forms are to the Divine Mind.

2 ~ **TWO** is the number of Her torches in many depictions. As a Goddess of liminality, Hekate is often bridging, yet separating, two places or two powers.

3 ~ **THREE** is the ultimate number for Hekate, three is most often associated to Her as we have seen so many depictions of Her with three faces or three bodies, beginning with the images

from Alkamenes in the 5th century BCE, and she is often addressed by epithets that refer to her triplicity or the triplicity of her powers: Triformis, Trimorphis, Trioditis, and Trivia. The last two epithets refer to Hekate as a Goddess of the crossroad, most often the meeting of three roads (versus the four-way crossroads often associated with Hermes). This three-way crossroads is not only the literal meeting place of three roads, but also the cosmological meeting place of three worlds - Sky, Earth, and the Sea - over which Hekate is granted power and influence in Hesiod's Theogony.

Her triplicity is reinforced by the association of Hekate with the Moon according to Porphyry:

> '...the Moon is Hekate, and is the symbol of her varying phases and of her power, which is dependent on those phases. For this reason, her power appears in three forms, the figure in white robes, golden sandals and lighted torches being the symbol of the new Moon. The basket, which she bears when she has mounted high, is the symbol of the cultivation of crops, which she causes to grow according to the increasing amount of light she gives. The symbol of the full Moon is the goddess wearing brazen sandals...'

In relation to the Moon, Hekate is part of a trinity consisting of Artemis, Selene and Herself. In the Chaldean Oracles, She is also one of three, being between the Divine Mind and the Demiurge.

4 ~ FOUR among the Neo-Platonists, four could be associated with Hekate as the Cosmic Soul in that the number four can be said to represent the force that organises and produces the material work through the four elements.

6 ~ SIX Nicomachus of Gessa identified the hexad (six) with the Cosmic Soul and even referred to the hexad as 'projection of Hekate'. Like the Cosmic Soul, in the number six opposites are brought into harmony which can be seen in the hexagram as a union of an upward and a downward pointing triangle.

9 ~ NINE The power of three multiplied by three. Plus, nine is the number associated with the moon (Yesod) in Qabala.

10 ~ TEN Like the number four, ten organises matter and also represents the delimiter of the world, like the Cosmic Soul.

12 ~ TWELVE In his discussion of Plato's *Republic*, Proclus connects the number twelve to Hekate in Her capacity as the Cosmic Soul:

> *'...twelve has the ability to bind together and harmonise diverse elements, whether they be of the individual body or the Cosmos; Twelve is the most complete boundary, resembling the causes that roll together the limits of the Cosmos...Therefore in the Laws (Plato) allotted the twelfth month to the worship of the chthonian deities, and the theologian says that the greatest goddess Hekate, who closes the boundaries of 'things within the Cosmos' and who, on account of this, is called 'Key-holder', was allotted the twelfth portion (of the Cosmos).'*

100 ~ ONE HUNDRED Suggested origin of the name Hekate is the word *Hekaton* that means *'one hundred'*.

334 ~ THREE HUNDRED-THIRTY FOUR In Greek Gematria, this is the number for Hekate, 'Εκατη'.

THE NUMBERS IN PRACTICE

The most significant number association is Three, the preeminent Hekatean number which connects to her through literature, art, and through her identification with the Cosmic Soul in the mysterious theurgic verses that comprise the *Chaldean Oracles*. These other numbers featured above seem to be quite a stretch compared to the many ways in which three is so closely identified with Hekate. In practice, we depict Hekate in threes and use three colours in our ritual spaces. In rituals to Hekate we may also chant and perform actions in threes. Also, giving offerings in threes is a powerful way to build a connection to her.

Two is a good number for candles or torches in the ritual space, especially when the priestess or priest identifies with the Goddess by holding one in each hand.

In my experience, the number twelve is the most suited to delimiting the magic circle, more so than ten, because twelve is divisible by three, four, two and six (other numbers bearing some relationship to Hekate). So much is contained in this number. It is also the number of the astrological signs, the ring of fixed stars that surround the earth and the solar system. For rites to Hekate as the Cosmic Soul, twelve lamps placed equidistant around the perimeter of the circle make it the boundary of the known Cosmos. Another approach to this is to make a twelve-side polygon within the circle.

In the use of symbols, though a foundation in established tradition through reference to literature and other sources is important, you may over time discover your own through personal gnosis and lead you beyond the known and documented lore.

Index

A

Acropolis, 121
Aegean, 113, 116
Aegina, 24
Ækáti, 107, 108, 109, 110, 111, 137, 138
Aeschylus, 148
Agora, 121
Akheilos, 92
Akkadians, 90
Alexandria, Clement of, 105, 106
Alkamenes, 170
Anatolia, 21, 22, 23, 31, 33, 35, 38, 43, 47
Anaxilas, 105
Anu, 91
Aphrodisia, 114
Aphrodite, 92, 116, 123
Apollo, 15, 20, 39, 48, 80
Apollonius of Tyana', 95
Apuleius, 96
Aradia, 10, 66
Ardennes, 16, 155, 158, 159
Aristides, Aelius, 93
Artemis, 17, 20, 34, 38, 47, 48, 110, 115, 117, 118, 119, 120, 142, 148, 170
Astarte, 16, 48
Ataecina, 45, 46, 47, 48, 49
Athens, 14, 21, 22, 34, 41, 64, 114, 115, 121, 124
Attis, 36
Australia, 157, 158, 160, 167
Axiokerse, 39

B

babies, 90, 91, 93, 94, 95, 98
Babylonian, 91
bay, 39
Belgium, 16, 155, 157, 158, 159, 161, 165
belly dance, 59, 101
Belos, 92, 96, 97
Belus, 92, 96, 97
blood, 37, 38, 39, 40, 41, 64, 70, 91, 94, 96
bloodletting, 38
Brimo, 38, 40, 104
Buddhism, 16, 127
bull, 31, 35, 37, 40, 42, 89, 110, 119, 121, 129, 130

C

Caesar, 40
Candomblé, 72, 73
canine, 91, *See* Dog
Castratos, 38
cat, 17, 39, 40
Çatalhöyük, 31, 32, 33, 35, 37
Cerberus, 118
Chaldean Oracles, 24, 30, 51, 81, 119, 128, 139, 140, 148, 169, 170, 171
Chalki, 114
Chaucer, 127
children, 16, 30, 33, 65, 76, 90, 91, 92, 93, 94, 95, 98, 110, 111, 112, 117, 120, 122, 123, 126, 143, 149, 162
Christian, 72, 105, 122, 149, 150
Chrysostom, Dio, 93, 96
Chthonia, 15, 116, 158
Cicero, 140
cinnamon, 39
Circe, 30, 149
Corinth, 113, 114
Cosmic Soul, 51, 140, 169, 170, 171, 172
Covenant of Hekate, 11, 14, 15, 17, 29, 49, 78
Crete, 37, 104, 119
Crone, 24, 147, 148, 149, 150, 151, 153
crossroads, 27, 29, 33, 44, 48, 52, 104, 108, 115, 118, 141, 143, 170
Crossroads, 26, 44, 71, 111, 113, 140, 159, 164, 168
Crowley, Aleister, 9, 30, 149, 150, 154
Cybele, 36, 37, 114, 130

D

d'Este, Sorita, 11, 19, 23, 29, 38, 52, 104,

105, 106, 153
daemones, 68, 141
dancing, 41, 59, 83, 157
dead, 32, 39, 40, 41, 55, 60, 63, 67, 95, 97, 98, 109, 112, 116, 120, 131, 132, 139, 156
deipna, 26
Delphi, 38, 39, 80, 93
Demeter, 21, 24, 25, 47, 119, 123, 130, 131, 148, 152, 153
demon, 84, 90, 94, 97, 98, 116, 123, 125
Diana, 17, 21, 47, 48, 55
Didima, 114
Dionysos, 10, 17, 36, 37, 38, 39, 41, 42, 129, 130, 131, 132, 133, 146
dog, 34, 35, 39, 42, 47, 89, 91, 106, 110, 111, 112, 118, 119, 137, 141
donkey, 91, 162
dreams, 76, 80, 81, 82, 83, 84, 85, 86, 87, 89, 109, 122, 139
Dreams, 24, 80, 81, 83, 85

E

Ecbatana, 47
egg, 164
Einalia, 116
Einalian, 15
Eleusinian Mysteries, 21, 140
Eleusis, 24, 42, 119, 152
Empousae, 90, 97
Enodia, 30
Ephesian Letters, 104, 105
Ephesus, 38, 47, 114
Epidaurus, 82, 114, 115, 120
Epipiridia, 121
epithets, 14, 23, 47, 114, 115, 116, 117, 119, 129, 138, 162, 164, 170
Erictho, 149
Europa, 119
Eurybatis, 93
Eusebius', 95

F

Fellowship of Isis, the, 81, 127
Filipopolis, 114
folklore, 17, 33, 51, 55, 84
Fortune, Dion, 150
frankincense, 39
Frazer, James, 9, 150, 153

G

Gallos, 38
Gematria, 171
Geneteira, 15
goat, 39, 46, 130, 149, 162
Golden Ass, 96
Golden Dawn, 9
Golden Fleece, 65, 131
Gorgon, 98
Gothla, 101, 103
Graves, Robert, 9, 98, 99, 150, 153
Greece, 14, 15, 22, 23, 34, 37, 61, 80, 90, 91, 99, 101, 102, 112, 114, 116, 121, 128, 129
Greek Magical Papyri, 30, 38, 39, 104, 106

H

Hades, 21, 120, 131, 140, 143
hags, 96
Hekate Triformis, 150
Hekaton, 171
Hekatos, 20, 22
Helios, 21, 65
Hephaestus, 118
Hephaistion, 92
Her Sacred Fires, 17, 29, 34, 35, 38, 153
Hera, 65, 92, 95, 96, 102, 120, 123, 130, 132, 146
hermaphrodite, 95
Hermes, 24, 39, 109, 116, 131, 135, 137, 139, 142, 144, 159, 164, 168, 170
Herne, 10
Hesiod, 21, 22, 31, 34, 92, 107, 116, 134, 136, 147, 151, 153, 170
Hestia, 120, 144
Hierophile, 92
Holy Mother, 122
honey, 36, 38, 64, 144
Horion, 144
Horned God, 37
household, 20, 26, 27, 28, 32, 91
Hunting, 120

I

Iacchos, 36, 41
Iberia, 44, 45, 47, 48
India, 160
interpretatio Graeca, 21

interpretatio Romano, 21
Ipemedeja, 34
Iran, 47
Iraq, 90
Isis, 20, 149

J

Janus, 142, 143, 148
jaws, 91, 92, 96

K

Keats, John, 99
Kirke. *See* Circe
Kirphis, Mount, 93
Korybantes, 37
Kos, 114
Kourotrophos, 20, 30, 95, 120
Krataiis, 15, 90
Krokos, 116
Kybele, 29, 31, 32, 33, 34, 35, 36, 37, 38, 40, 41, 42, 148

L

Lagina, 22, 23, 33, 34, 113, 119
Lamashtu, 90, 91, 95, 96, 97, 98
Lamassu, 90
Lamia, 30, 90, 92, 93, 94, 95, 96, 97, 98, 99, 102, 103
Lamia, the, 90, 91, 92, 93, 95, 97, 100, 101
leopard, 31, 35, 36, 43
Levant, 23, 44
Libya, 92, 93, 96, 102
Lilith, 91, 99
Linear B, 34
lion, 31, 34, 35, 36
lionesses, 91
Lucan, 149
Lug, 48
Lugus, 48

M

Macbeth, 50, 51, 149, 154
Maenads, 36
magic, 9, 11, 13, 15, 16, 17, 19, 24, 33, 38, 40, 42, 50, 60, 66, 69, 73, 75, 76, 128, 138, 149, 164, 172
Magna Mater, 23, 38

maiden, 95, 111, 148
Maiden, 24, 111, 147, 148, 151
Makhates, 95
Matar, 32, 33
Medea, 13, 19, 30, 55, 60, 62, 64, 65, 66, 67, 68, 69, 70, 149
Medeia. *See* Medea
Menippus, 95
Mesopotamia, 23, 47, 90, 100
Middle Sky, 109, 138
Miletus, 22, 33
milk, 38, 42, 64, 129, 130, 144
Minoan, 35, 37, 90, 91, 98, 119
Minotaur, 37
moon, 55, 56, 60, 65, 109, 138, 139, 143, 157, 164, 165, 171
Moonchild, 30, 149
Mormo, 98
Mother of Gods, 30, 33, 148
Mother of the Gods, 32, 142, 143
myrtle, 39

N

necromancy, 149
necromantic, 149
Neoplatonism, 113, 119
Nicomachus, 170
nine, 171
Nonnus, 35, 36, 42

O

oak, 160
Oceanic Hekate, 15
Ogden, Daniel, 101
Olympus, 121
oracles, 80, 81, 92
Oracles, 24, 25, 80, 142
Origen, 105
Orphic, 13, 21, 28, 37, 104, 107, 112, 113, 116, 119, 127, 128, 129, 130, 131, 132, 134, 136, 137, 138, 141, 144, 148, 154
Orphic Hymns, 37, 113, 116, 131
Ourania, 116
Ovid, 55, 60

P

Pærsæphóni, 107
Pan, 9, 10

Panathenaicus, 93
Parthenon, 121
Pasiphae, 37
Pausanias, 22, 90, 92
Pausanius, 21
Pella, 114
Peloponnese, 114
Persephone, 21, 47, 48, 119, 120, 129, 131, 132, 133, 148
Persia, 23
PGM, 9, 38, 39, 40, 41, 104, 148, 149
Pharsalia, 149
Philebus, 139, 141
Phillinon, 95
Philostratus, 95, 96, 99
Phoenicia, 23
Phorkys, 92
Phosphoros, 15, 18, 20
pig, 91
Pindar, 148
Plato, 127, 134, 139, 140, 141, 169, 171
Ploutohn, 107, 131
Plutarch, 26, 94, 96, 97, 99, 100, 105, 139, 141
Poseidon, 92, 123, 124, 137
pregnant, 35, 91, 95, 133
Propylaia, 21
Proserpina, 47
Prostaterius, 144
Psyche, 169
psychopomp, 30, 32, 42, 131, 142

Q

Qabala, 171

R

Restless Dead, 19, 24, 29, 99
Rexchthon, 155, 166, 167
Rhea, 30, 33, 36, 37, 117, 142, 148
Rhodes, 65, 114
Rite of Her Sacred Fires, 48, 71, 77, 105
Roads, 112, 115
Roman, 12, 15, 21, 33, 35, 47, 48, 72, 99, 100, 113, 142, 149, 150
Rome, 23, 34, 38, 40, 129
Rose, 144
royal, 31, 114, 116

S

saffron, 108, 111, 112, 116, 144
Samos, 93, 114
Samothrace, 24, 38, 119
Samothraki, 114
sandals, 91, 170
Santorini, 116
Scylla, 30, 90, 92, 96, 98
sea, 14, 31, 42, 52, 56, 108, 109, 111, 112, 114, 116, 131, 135, 136, 137, 138, 139, 149
Sea Priestess, 150
Sekhmet, 81
Selene, 30, 39, 47, 148, 170
Selinunte, 22
sex, 40
Shakespeare, William, 14, 50, 51, 53, 54, 55, 127, 149, 154
shapeshift, 36
shark, 92, 96, 102
Shekinah, 17, 53
Sicily, 22, 48, 51, 80
Siculus, Diodorus, 93
snake, 91, 98
Sokrates, 134, 139, 141
solar, 88, 172
Sophia, 53
Soteira, 18, 20, 51, 52, 128, 131, 132, 146, 153
Stesichorus, 90, 92
Stratonikea, 113, 120
Stromata, 105
succubus, 84, 90, 96
Supper, 26

T

Tartarus, 124
Theogony, 21, 22, 31, 32, 116, 136, 138, 147, 151, 153, 170
Thera, 116
Thessaly, 69, 114, 119, 129, 149
Thrace, 23
throne, 31, 34
Timaeus, 140, 169
Timeaus, 140
Titans, 116, 132, 133, 136, 148
Triformis, 47, 170
Trimorphis, 170
Trioditis, 170

Trivia, 21, 170
Türkiye, 22, 23

V

Valiente, Doreen, 10
vampires, 98
Vergina, 114
Virtue, 107, 137

W

Wicca, 13, 14, 15, 75, 78, 127, 154
Windsor, 10
Wine, 144, 146
Witch, 149
witchcraft, 9, 13, 14, 15, 19, 24, 69, 74, 75, 76, 78, 116, 128, 138, 149
witches, 29, 51, 60, 66, 69, 75, 96, 101, 103, 149, 158
wizards, 101, 103
wolf, 91
World Soul, 29, 31, 51, 52, 119, 128, 139, 140, 142, 144, 169

Y

Yesod, 171
Yoga, 127

Z

Zagreus, 36, 37, 132, 133
Zeus, 92, 95, 96, 116, 119, 123, 130, 132, 133, 135, 136, 137, 142, 143, 152

www.avaloniabooks.com

www.ingramcontent.com/pod-product-compliance
Lightning Source LLC
Chambersburg PA
CBHW011949150426

43194CB00017B/2847